CLEVELAND
NEIGHBORHOOD
GUIDEBOOK

EDITED BY THE STAFF OF BELT MAGAZINE

First Edition 2016.

ISBN: 978-0-9968367-2-2

Belt Publishing
1667 E. 40th Street #1G1
Cleveland, Ohio 44120
www.beltmag.com

Book design by Meredith Pangrace
Cover illustration by David Wilson

ALSO BY BELT PUBLISHING:

Rust Belt Chic: The Cleveland Anthology

A Detroit Anthology

The Cincinnati Anthology

Car Bombs to Cookie Tables: The Youngstown Anthology

The Pittsburgh Anthology

How To Live In Detroit Without Being A Jackass

Happy Anyway: A Flint Anthology

Forthcoming in 2016:

The Akron Anthology

The Buffalo Anthology

How To Talk Midwestern

TABLE OF CONTENTS

WRITINGS:

LAKE ERIE

THE FLATS

LAKEWOOD

DETROIT SHOREWAY

OHIO CITY

TREMONT

cleveland

BROOKLYN CENTRE

PARMA

EUCLID

 COLLINWOOD

 EAST CLEVELAND

 GLENVILLE

ST.CLAIR SUPERIOR

GOODRICH-KIRTLAND PARK HOUGH

 SOUTH EUCLID

CLEVELAND HEIGHTS

LITTLE ITALY

KINSMAN

 LARCHMERE

 SHAKER HEIGHTS

SLAVIC VILLAGE

ohio

MOUNT PLEASANT

 LEE-MILES

INTRODUCTION

Spend enough time reading "Best of Cleveland" listicles on the internet or browsing tourist brochures, and an image of Cleveland will likely form: a place with music, art, beer, ballgames, and skyscrapers filled with down-to-earth folks. It is a fine image and one that is connected to reality: there are few things better than a day spent at the West Side Market and the Cleveland Museum of Art followed by drinks in Ohio City overlooking Terminal Tower, and on such a day you may well find yourself surrounded by happy, shiny Clevelanders.

But that is also only one picture of Cleveland, and as with so much else of late, Cleveland tourism has become a story of haves and have nots: some places get all the clicks. This is where this book comes in. We wanted to pan out, look to the sides, and show other Clevelands, too — to let shine the hidden gems, stop to note the cracked glass, and poke into the shadows of what has been lost.

When we thought about how best to tell the story of Cleveland neighborhoods, we decided to canvass the block. We invited stories. Send us essays about your neighborhoods, we asked. It can be a pretty story or an ugly story, a tale from the past or a glimpse of the future. We did not define "neighborhood" (a corner? a ward district? a conclave of a certain demographic?) but let those interested in participating do that themselves. And then we read, delighted, as people from South Euclid and New York and Larchmere and Boston submitted essays that lit up the corners, alleys and bike lanes of the city and inner-ring suburbs.

The result—the essays in this book—is more kaleidoscopic than Photoshopped. If you want to learn more about downtown, this book is not for you. This book is for those who want to understand the streets that radiate away from Terminal Tower, and who understand that as pretty as the city often is, it can sometimes be ugly. You will read about places no longer here, such as the Little Italy Historical Museum, and League

Park, as well as increasingly popular areas such as North Collinwood and Asiatown. You will learn about Cleveland Heights' natural history, Mount Pleasant back in the day, and Opportunity Corridors missed. The writers will tell you stories about starting a business in Ohio City, first-time homebuying in Detroit Shoreway, the unjustified self-loathing of South Euclid, troubling developments in Tremont, closed schools in Lee-Miles, and a vineyard in Hough. Bound together, the essays portray a Cleveland as complex as its residents.

In between these essays we laced some surprises, aimed both at our increasing numbers of tourists (hi!) and residents looking for something new to do: *Belt Magazine* Editors' Picks for the best restaurants, dive bars, housing deals, breakfasts, and more. We also feature recommendations written by local experts on their picks for the city's best nature, art, and music. We bet you will disagree with some choices, and we look forward to discussing those with you, perhaps over Chinese in St. Clair Superior or cocktails in Duck Island.

It is impossible to put together such a book and also be truly "representative" or "comprehensive," so fair warning: there are stories of neighborhoods left untold and voices unheard within these pages. Perhaps a more accurate title would be "A Partial, Good-Faith but Not Nearly Comprehensive Enough Cleveland Neighborhood Guidebook." We intend to keep filling in the gaps and add more pins to our map, at our online home, *Belt Magazine* (beltmag.com), where we are always eager to publish Cleveland's stories.

Thanks to all the writers and sponsors for enabling the making of this book—and here's to you, dear readers, for closing the circle by hearing these stories, thus completing this new story of Cleveland. We hope to see you soon, somewhere around town.

Losing Lakewood

SALLY ERRICO

I moved to Lakewood a few weeks after breaking up with my boyfriend and, not coincidentally, a few weeks after I started sleeping with Adam. My boyfriend and I had lived together on the east side—his native stomping ground—and as soon as the first winter hit, I became desperate to leave.

"You realize the snowbelt that goes all the way to Buffalo starts here, right? Like, specifically here. If we lived 20 minutes west, we'd have an entirely different climate."

"I like the east side. Now hand me the ice scraper."

There were other reasons for moving to Lakewood. It seemed to me a city in the best possible ways: progressive in both its politics and its society, a place where a proud Cleveland met a cultured liberalism. It was full of shops and restaurants and bars, and their interconnectedness—the sheer number of them and their proximity to one another, and to residential streets, and to Cleveland itself—was to me a characteristic of what urban life should be.

On a more practical level, Lakewood was also where Adam lived. I met him at a party in December, and when he mentioned that he and his girlfriend would be moving in together in May, I thought, I have six months to make you fall in love with me. I had known him for an hour. The intensity of my attraction was unlike anything I'd ever felt: He was tall, slim, and impeccably dressed, with curly brown hair and eyes so dark they were almost black. As we got to know each other better over the next few months, I also discovered he was sometimes vain. He could be jealous and resentful. But his flaws made him more appealing, which is why I maintain that my attraction wasn't just physical. I was in love.

The situation was complicated by 1) my boyfriend and 2) Adam's girlfriend. For a while, I imagined that Adam and I could just…hang out together forever, complacent in our respective relationships, no rocking of boats. We had mutual friends, so there was always an excuse to see each other; we enjoyed the same things, so if we happened to find ourselves at, say, the same concert, hey, what a coincidence! But then one night, after we attended a wine-fueled fundraiser for the Cleveland Public Theatre, he kissed me. I was living in Lakewood by the end of the month.

I found my apartment by driving around and looking for "For Rent" signs in the windows of buildings (it was a kinder, simpler, realty app–free time: 2004). I checked out houses, duplexes, and apartment complexes, some near the lake and others closer to the airport, some beautiful and others one leak away from being condemned. When I called the number in the window of a building on the corner of Detroit and Riverside, the owner said he could show me a one-bedroom immediately—he was there now, renovating it. For $525 a month, it was mine.

The neighborhood was everything. I could go to the dry cleaner and the liquor store on the same walk. Sushi, falafel, and pizza were just a short drive up Detroit. And if funds were low, so were prices at Marc's, that T.J. Maxx of food, with its dented tuna cans and inexplicably large selection of peanut butter. Stores and restaurants flew rainbow flags year-round, and the one business I knew of that was openly homophobic—a taxidermy shop that appeared closed even when it was open and had a bumper sticker reading "God made Adam and Eve, not Adam and Steve" in the window—was also openly mocked. I could go for a morning run in the Metropark, and in the evening, have a glass of wine at Three Birds. By comparison, my hometown near Cedar Point had not one single store at which to buy a CD, and there was opposition to plans for a Taco Bell because the locals believed it would attract gangs. Lakewood was a Shangri-La.

And just off of Detroit: Adam's apartment, the seat of both my joy and misery. He hadn't broken up with his girlfriend yet, but soon, I just knew, it would happen. They'd never have the chance to move in together. In the meantime, my plan was simple: continue sleeping with him and wait for him to give in to our obvious chemistry. But I'd forget this on the days when I'd drive past his street on my way home from work and see his girlfriend's car parked in front of his building. Her carrrrrrr! I would be in agony as I pulled into my parking lot, imagining them in a Kama Sutra's worth of positions—or worse, doing something like making dinner, throwing little puffs of flour at each other and laughing, a scene straight out of some stupid rom-com. I'd drag myself up the stairs of my building, collapsing in tears on the slipcovered couch that had been a hand-me-down from my grandparents.

This, as it turns out, is not a way to build self-esteem. I recognized that I'd become the kind of woman I'd always pitied, the "crazy" one waiting for a kind word or sign of affection from an emotionally (and otherwise) unavailable man. But I didn't know how to break out. I'd decide that I was done, that I was too disgusted with myself to continue, and I'd go on dates with other guys. But then Adam would call, and the adrenaline would flood me.

Complete escape seemed the only option. For years, I'd entertained the fantasy of moving to New York City—a giant Lakewood!—and I began to plan in earnest. It was both a distraction and a bluff: I was sure Adam would stop me. Our relationship wasn't just sex, after all. We'd been friends before we'd been anything, and we'd spent nights talking about our lives, our ambitions, our secrets. That had to count for something.

I packed my apartment slowly, waiting. He never came. I got in the van and left Lakewood, this time by taking Detroit across the bridge and into Rocky River. I didn't want to drive down the streets we'd walked, or pass the diner where we'd sat across from each other in squeaky vinyl booths, talking over coffee until 4 a.m. More than anything, I didn't want to see his building. I felt at the time that he had taken Lakewood from me, but now, of course, I understand that I was the thief, and a cowardly one at that. I was leaving the only apartment I'd ever have that would be just mine: no roommates, no boyfriends. I'd been too obsessed with my heartbreak to allow myself the pleasure of being a single 24-year-old woman in a city that I loved.

I later learned that Adam's girlfriend had been cheating on him all along. They had broken up right around the time I'd settled in New York, where every street had been full of things I wanted to tell him about and every face was that of a stranger. ◀

Best Deservedly Spendy Restaurants

The restaurants that rightly receive the most national acclaim are **Greenhouse Tavern** (or anyplace by chef Jonathon Sawyer), **Dante** (or anyplace by chef Dante Bocuzzi) and **Lola** (or anyplace by chef Michael Symon throughout the area).

Flying Fig Karen Small was an early adopter of both locally sourced food and Ohio City, and the restaurant remains consistently superb.

L'Alabatros is brasserie French at its best—go after the orchestra, and be sure to order the French Toast.

Pier W in Lakewood is the epitome of both midcentury décor and lakeside dining. Their elaborate brunch may be the best place in town to observe a wide swath of Cleveland's demographic celebrating.

EDWINS is not just an inventive, heroic experiment in offering formerly incarcerated adults a trade and a job—it is also the spot for classic French haute cuisine in town, especially when the patio is open.

fire food & drink With EDWINS on Shaker Square is Douglas Katz' flagship restaurant. It is always buzzing with locals from Shaker Heights and points east, and the superb pizza appetizers are big enough for an entrée.

Still hungry? Here are five great independently owned upscale restaurants to try: **Toast**, **Spice**, **Alley Cat**, **Felice** and **Fat Cats**.

We Are Good in Glenville:

A Visit to the Honey Do Club Neighborhood Bar

KATHRINE MORRIS

Cleveland is a city of neighborhoods. Each tells a story with its own unique culture and history, the restaurant you have to eat at, and of course, a neighborhood bar. Being a Glenville resident my entire life, one would assume that I have ventured to my own neighborhood bar before 2015. On a Friday night when most of the city is leaving their distinctive neighborhoods to venture to the melting pot of fun in downtown Cleveland, we found ourselves on the northern side of Glenville's boundaries at a small, quirky, corner bar on St. Clair Ave. called "The Honey Do Club."

Walking into the bar, we were warmly greeted by an assortment of neighborly drinkers who welcomed new faces into their home. This is truly home for the regulars. Everyone who crossed the threshold got a loud, boisterous; "HEY Y'ALL," accompanied by an open-armed hug from Sonny, the barmaid, who has been a staple at The Honey Do. "Sonny knows everyone who comes in here and she'll get you right on the drinks."

First impressions: this is not your TownHall or Barley House and it doesn't have to be. The storefront bar which sits under an apartment suite on the corner of St. Clair and Vashti Ave is a dive bar in every sense and has the character of a neighborhood bar your average downtown Cleveland bar lacks, one being that it is extremely local. It serves the people who live within walking distance and those people know each other well enough to continue previous conversations from the night before and reminisce on the old times in Glenville. There are no fancy named cocktails and the bar prices are reasonable enough for all the regulars to be able to enjoy themselves without checking their bank statements at the end of the night.

Staff: the staff was overwhelmingly friendly. The owner, Maria Roscoe, has owned the establishment for over 15 years and Sonny, the friendly barmaid, has worked at the bar over a decade. The Honey Do Club is Glenville's "Cheers," as one person put it. Everyone knows who you are, what your favorite drink is and of course, your name. Sonny enthusiastically poured us double shots of top shelf liquor as she told us stories of her family's heritage, her experiences at the Honey Do

Club over the many years she's worked there and her love for everyone who comes in the bar, even going on to say "…we're all family here, that's why people keep coming here."

People: everyone is different. A family of different personalities intertwined in one place at the same time. It's a little overwhelming at first, until you realize that the yelling man across the bar looks like your uncle and he's yelling at your cousin and it all makes sense. The bar is full of colorful personalities that blend together organically. At its most crowded, the bar was packed from front to back with 100+ people laughing, joking, and having a good time. Even in the shotgun style bar, with little room to accommodate, dancing is so important the patrons somehow make it work. At one point an older man began doing splits down the bar, clutching his drink tightly while the crowd cheered him on.

There is definitely a lure to neighborhood bars. They encourage neighbors to be neighbors, they create and foster bonds and most of all, they keep culture strong. The Honey Do Club is an old place with a family feel and it is the locals in Glenville who keep the bar thriving and colorful. It's a local, laid-back, and no fuss type of place that allows you to feel embraced as soon as you walk in. Glenville loves its culture and its people. As a lifelong resident of Glenville I loved being in an environment where I was around my neighbors from down the street, drinking and sharing stories of Glenville's past and future. If you are looking for a true feeling of culture, without the top 40 pop and fancy named drinks, this might be the place for you. The past and future of Glenville, though, will continue to center around the cultural places like the Honey Do provides. Suffice it to say, we are good in Glenville. ◄

Best Neighborhood Bars

What holds a neighborhood together better than a bar? Every good neighborhood has a place where neighbors can gather for a beer or three. Some comfort food can boost the value even more.

Millard Fillmore Presidential Library Tell people you are going there and if they don't know better, you'll seem intellectual, but better yet, you also get great beer options, live entertainment, and some basic food.

The Tavern Company Reasonably priced everything, killer burgers, a strong tap presence, and a family feel.

Old Angle Tavern In the heart of the W. 25th St. brewery scene, Old Angle sticks with what it does best: beer, soccer, food, and good service.

Muldoon's Saloon & Eatery A classic example of a neighborhood bar. Big space, robust food and drink menu, and a party room.

Platform Brewery Great local brews (and guest brews too) in a location light on a neighborhood focal point. Plenty of space, TVs, rotating food options, and outdoor patio.

Stone Mad Pub The building was originally a bar back in 1912, and Stone Mad embraces that past with modern twists. Good food and drink, bocce, and a spacious stone patio.

Gigi's On Fairmount Perhaps a bit more "upscale" than one would expect from a neighborhood bar, but there's nothing wrong with that. Great food, wine, cozy atmosphere.

Johnny Mango World Café & Bar The margaritas are enough to lure you in, but the food is worth mentioning as well — Mexican/Asian/Creole/etc. will keep your tastebuds in a state of happy confusion.

Tremont:

A Product of Its Past, a Piece of Its Future

TARA VANTA

Originally known as Brooklyn Heights, before it was incorporated into Ohio City between 1836 and 1854, the neighborhood of Tremont was finally annexed by Cleveland in 1867—and since then it's had almost as many names as it's had identities. After 1867, the development of Cleveland's first institution of higher learning shifted Tremont's name from Cleveland Heights to University Heights; its role as the location for two Union army camps during the Civil War converted this label to Lincoln Heights; and the 1910 establishment of Tremont Elementary resulted in today's handle, "Tremont."

Tremont's economic peaks and valleys have defined it since the Civil War, when the area found itself in a perfect position to meet the growing demand for wartime goods. Its central location was key to its success. The ability to import and export materials and products via the Cuyahoga River and the Erie Railroad gave Tremont a leg up on the competition; so did its steady influx of cheap, immigrant labor. The 1862 establishment of Camp Cleveland, Cleveland's largest and best-developed Civil War camp, was the final factor in this equation. Providing for the 15,230 military men that came through Camp Cleveland set Tremont's economic boom into full swing. By 1865, more than half of the iron ore extracted from Lake Superior came through Cleveland and 44 percent of all ships used on the Great Lakes were assembled locally.

Both Tremont's population and industry grew rapidly for a number of years. Local access to raw materials, transportation, and immigrant labor all converged to draw in major manufacturing companies like Lamson & Sessions electrical products. These companies facilitated even further growth and played a significant role in sustaining Tremont's economy after the war, even through World War I and the Great Depression, until World War II ushered in another area of industrially driven prominence.

Prior to 1830 Tremont was slow-growing, but the localization economy catalyzed a sustained period of growth: Irish men and women flooded the area in the 1860s to aid in the construction of the Ohio and Erie Canals; Poles flocked to Tremont in the late 1890s and constituted over 50 percent of U.S Steel Corporation's workforce by 1919; excess labor demand was eagerly met by Greek migrants in the early

1900s, and later, by surges of Ukrainians and Hispanics, who arrived in the 1950s and 60s.

But though these groups produced coworkers, their day-to-day lives were significantly less interwoven. Tremont's Polish settlement, Kantowo, is one of the many ethnically separate niches to result. By 1900 there were 32 Polish grocery stores and 67 Polish saloons in Cleveland, and Poles' entrepreneurial endeavors largely targeted those with similar culture, not the community as a whole. Similar tendencies marked the Greek, Ukrainian, and Puerto Rican communities. Religious anchors were often considered to be the cornerstone of this insulation, as enclaves served many positive community functions. The Spanish Assembly of God, for example, was founded on West 11th Street in 1952, and by 1995 two-thirds of Cleveland-area Puerto Ricans resided between W 5th St. and W 65th St. Although the actual distance between these groups was minimal, the social separation between them was significant.

The separation forced on Tremont residents by the midcentury closing of the Central Viaduct Bridge and the construction of Interstates 71 and 490 was also significant, to say the least. The Central Viaduct, constructed in 1888, connected Tremont to the east bank of the Cuyahoga River and provided a vital connection to downtown, giving residents of Tremont easy access to institutions and businesses in the city, resulting in a time of rapid growth. Unfortunately for Tremont, this growth was abruptly stunted when the Central Viaduct was deemed unsafe in 1941 and demolished in 1942. With plans for its replacement still several years off, the impact was immense. Newspaper columnist Robert H. Clifford highlighted the laundry list of ramifications: "A 'CITY' of nearly 30,000 persons virtually isolated. Serious bottlenecking of traffic arteries…endless inconvenience for thousands of workers…threatened collapse of a whole section's business. These are the problems faced by Cleveland's Seventh Ward."

Tremont would have likely been able to weather the closing of the Viaduct alone, but the subsequent construction of Cleveland's interstate system gave rise to a period of acute regional decline. Interstates 71 and 490 tore through the neighborhood, displacing upwards of 19,000 residents by 1975. Tremont's newfound isolation and consequent decline in economic opportunity prompted many to permanently flee the area. Tremont's population dropped from 36,686 in 1920 to a mere 10,304 by 1980. Steve Rugare, of the Cleveland Urban Design Collaborative, described the situation thusly: "The freeways simply ploughed through the existing fabric, leaving isolated enclaves to subsequent decay...commercial streets were cut off from nearby residents, and children were forced to walk exposed pedestrian overpasses to get to basic services like schools and parks." The consequences of the highway construction were incapacitating. Lost jobs and residential disturbances induced flight from the area. Those who remained were generally those who could not afford to relocate. Neighborhood tax bases declined and property maintenance fell by the wayside. The Plain Dealer commented on this downward spiral, "Tremont changed . . . here and there the neighborhood began to crumble. Vandals destroyed house after house, and arson took its toll." The article suggested that the remaining residents were largely unemployed, undereducated renters and that neighborhood demographics were shifting, In 1999, 23.19 percent of Tremont's population earned less than $10,000 a year. The community organizations that were about to intervene had their work cut out for them.

Merrick House is one such organization. Founded in 1919, Merrick House's initial mission was to provide recreational and cultural activities for young immigrants, but in the tumultuous decades that followed, this role expanded to encompass the facilitation of career guidance for women, assistance for unwed mothers, free dental care, and support for the passage of beneficial neighborhood legislation, amongst other things. Merrick House's role as a community anchor helped Tremont residents to bear the worst of times, but Merrick was not content only to provide support. Merrick House acknowledged the importance of reversing Tremont's rough image to salvage its future, so in 1979 they established the Tremont West Development Corporation to do so.

Tremont West Development Corporation (TWDC) is a not-for-profit citizens group that has done its best to reconstitute what used to make Tremont a great place to live. TWDC has helped Tremont to essentially rebrand itself and this reinvention has been accompanied by substantial benefits. In 1989 not a single household in Tremont's central block group earned more than $75,000 annually, but ten years later, eleven households earned between $75,000 and $99,999, seven earned between $100,000 and $124,999, and seven others earned more than $150,000. That said, 63.1 percent of Tremont's residents still earned less than $24,999 in the same year. The neighborhood was heading in the right direction, but equity issues were still apparent. TWDC's wins can be attributed to the fact that the group wisely homed in on the three largest components of Tremont's original deterioration: first, TWDC tried to make the highway debacle right by upping the quality and quantity of Tremont's housing stock; second, they made headway earning back the community's trust with crime prevention efforts; and finally, have attacked the downward spiral of the economy head on with business development projects that have both produced jobs and enhanced Tremont's tax base.

Tremont today finds itself at an interesting crossroads. The neighborhood has advanced through nearly every stage of the "suburban neighborhood lifecycle." Albeit slightly skewed from the current image of "suburbia," Tremont's initial incursion of well-off inhabitants outside of the city could certainly be deemed a form of "suburbanization"; "infilling" occurred via accelerated civil war immigration; "downgrading" was forced due to transportation obstacles; "thinning out" was an inevitable byproduct of Tremont's stunted economy; and TWDC has made significant strides towards neighborhood "renewal." Beginning in the 1970s and 1980s, many artists were drawn to Tremont by its old-world feel, ornate architecture, affordable housing, and downtown views. These individuals marked the beginning of what has become an expanding neighborhood of art galleries, eateries, boutiques, new condos, and rehabilitated homes. Select corridors and select residents of Tremont are thriving today. But alas, that sums up the challenge moving forward. Evolving in a way that respects its heritage, particularly the people, will be key to Tremont's continued success. Tremont needs to be a neighborhood first and foremost. It needs to be a responsible steward to all of its residents. It does not need to create the next shiny thing. ◀

Best Coffee Shops

The staff of *Belt Magazine* must admit to frequenting the city's coffee shops to take advantage of free Wi-Fi, good music, friendly baristas, and freshly roasted beans. Here are our most common haunts.

Phoenix Coffee The standard-bearer for locally owned coffee shops, Phoenix has several locations around the city. Try the speedball if you need an extra jolt.

Rising Star In an renovated firehouse, Rising Star is popular with west side hipsters and caffeine afficionados.

Pour Not your father's downtown coffee shop, Pour has quickly become the place for business people to do deals over cups of joe.

Loop The best place in town to mix coffee drinking with vinyl record shopping, Loop's bright windows make even winter days warm.

Civilization Tremont's long-standing, more-cozy-than-hip spot with both delicious baked goods and outdoor seating.

Blackbird Baking Company Tucked away in a small storefront in Lakewood, Blackbird Baking Company serves some of the area's best pastries.

A Walk Through North Collinwood

BENNO MARTENS

The Beachland Ballroom is a crowd of people and noise. But there is no band on stage at the iconic music venue on Waterloo Road in Cleveland's North Collinwood neighborhood. No crunching guitars, rapid-fire drums, or melodic vocals. The place is abuzz for a very different reason: Saturday brunch.

I'm seated at the bar, with a Southern-fried buttermilk chicken and biscuit sandwich in front of me, reveling in the positive energy that permeates the space on a January afternoon. Seated next to me is Daniel Subwick, a resident of North Collinwood who moved into the Glencove Building on East 156th Street in August 2015.

"This is the place to be on the east side [of Cleveland]," he says as we talk. "You don't have to compromise in North Collinwood. The scene is here."

The Glencove is a first-of-its-kind experiment in Cleveland, being spearheaded by Northeast Shores Development Corporation, the nonprofit community development organization that serves the North Collinwood neighborhood. Northeast Shores redeveloped the building, a former tavern, into apartments and artist studios/gallery spaces.

Tenants of the Glencove pay extremely affordable rents, and are required to contribute to the maintenance of the interior and exterior of the property and to attend community meetings. In exchange, they earn equity—as much as $10,000 if they stay for 10 years—which can then be used however the tenant wishes. The hope of Northeast Shores is that the program will build a bond between the residents and the neighborhood, and that they will use the equity they amass for a down payment on a home or gallery in North Collinwood.

"The program fits perfectly for where I am in my life," Subwick says. "It helped me to immediately get involved in the community, and getting that equity at the end of the day will just be a huge bonus."

Because of the community involvement feature of the program, the residents of the Glencove have been able to get to know one another much more quickly than in a normal apartment building.

"It's become like a little family," he says. "For example, Maura Rogers, a musician who lives in the building, has her practice space directly below my apartment. Her band, Maura Rogers and the Bellows, is so good, I would never even think to complain about the noise. I get my own private concerts every time they practice."

Subwick, who serves in the Housing Department of an inner-ring Cleveland suburb and feeds his creativity through music and web design, is exactly the type of young professional that every rebuilding neighborhood should be clamoring for. Engaged in the community and a strong supporter of local businesses, he is enamored with what North Collinwood has to offer.

"You get the sense of community really quickly," he says as we walk down Waterloo Road. "There are a lot of people who are really excited to be living here."

Walking around the neighborhood, there is a sense of optimism in the air. A new streetscaping project was completed in the autumn of 2014 on Waterloo Road, making for a pleasurable pedestrian experience. There are art galleries at every turn, including the much-lauded Waterloo Arts Gallery and the Maria Neil Art Project, and a wide variety of new business development. During our stroll, we pass the following:

- an upscale watering hole amusingly named the Millard Fillmore Presidential Library;
- a recently opened pizza parlor called Citizen Pie;
- two record stores(!), Music Saves and Blue Arrow Records;
- a bakery named Cakes by Sweetwater;
- the Native Cleveland store, a boutique shop featuring unique Cleveland-related paraphernalia, all made in Cleveland or by former Clevelanders;
- a yet-to-be opened coffee shop called Six Shooter Coffee Roasters that seems to be closing in on the end of construction;

And all of that doesn't even mention the fact that we're standing less than a mile from the shores of Lake Erie. North Collinwood boasts nearly three miles of shoreline, an asset that as of now is still underutilized.

"That's the next pressure point," Subwick says. "Connecting what's going on here on Waterloo with the lake is hugely important. The lake is an asset that could pull the whole neighborhood together, complement the existing arts and culture, and really become a magnet for new residents and investment."

Rounding the corner of Waterloo and East 161st Street, Subwick ushers me into Brick Ceramic and Design Studio, a ceramics studio and gallery that offers classes and open studio time to area residents, as well as its own commercial work. Brick was founded by Valerie Grossman, a ceramics artist and graduate of the Cleveland Institute of Art.

"This isn't the kind of place you find in every neighborhood," he tells me. "[North Collinwood] is the perfect venue. There's no pretentiousness. The artists are here, period, and they'd be doing their thing regardless. But it's great to have places in the neighborhood like this."

We head back in the direction of the Beachland to have a beer and talk a little more, and run into one of Subwick's neighbors at the Glencove, a photographer, on the street outside. The two are genuinely excited to see each other.

"I've never lived anywhere else where I could connect with everyone in my building, not just on an artistic level, but on a personal one," Subwick tells me once we're back inside.

Originally built in 1950 to house the Croatian Library Home, the Beachland Ballroom has been operating as a music venue in the North Collinwood neighborhood since 2000.

"This place is the anchor of the neighborhood, for sure," Subwick says. "Without it, you'd lose that central, driving force. Everything has grown organically around it."

After the devastation wrought by the housing crisis and economic downturn, that anchor, along with the work of Northeast Shores, has helped North Collinwood to hang on for dear life. A fortunate few areas in Cleveland have succeeded in bringing themselves back from the brink of oblivion, and North Collinwood is one place that has quietly been doing just that.

Not often mentioned alongside the likes of Ohio City and Detroit Shoreway, North Collinwood is at the forefront of neighborhood redevelopment in the city. Utilizing the arts, targeted investment, and an innovative renter equity program that could certainly be replicated elsewhere in the neighborhood and the city at large, North Collinwood has begun to symbolize the very best Cleveland has to offer.

"I already feel it, wanting to stay in this neighborhood long-term," Subwick says. "There's a great relationship between the people here, a ton of friendliness and support. It's really beautiful." ◄

Best Places for Live Music

BY ANNIE ZALESKI
Freelance music writer

Cleveland's a music town through and through. Need proof? Its vibrant live music venues are a reflection of the city's diversity, history, and proud cultural heritage.

Beachland Ballroom A former Croatian Hall, this two-room venue—a roomy Ballroom and a homey Tavern—brings rock, soul, folk, punk, and everything else in between to the proud Waterloo neighborhood.

Mahall's 20 Lanes This refurbished 1920s bowling alley holds rock, punk, and comedy shows in two places: downstairs, right across the hall from their basement lanes, and upstairs in an expansive room just across the lobby from a well-stocked, well-curated bar.

Grog Shop Since 1992, unpretentious Coventry anchor the Grog Shop has brought the best up-and-coming rock and hip-hop acts to Cleveland.

Barking Spider This hidden University Circle gem is a musician's haven, a cozy bar that ensures songwriters have an attentive audience (and a well-filled tip jar) whenever they perform.

Parkview Nite Club Detroit Shoreway's venerable live music bar boasts an unparalleled comfort food menu and some of the grittiest, most dynamic blues acts around.

Bop Stop at the Music Settlement The near west side now has its own destination for all things jazz—whether it's experimental and avant-leaning performers, or musicians who take a more traditional approach.

Wade Oval Wednesdays University Circle is hopping even more in the summer, when local bands perform outdoors as part of the annual mid-week, after-work concert series.

The Paris
of Cleveland

SAM MCNULTY

first visited Ohio City in the early '80s with my parents and six siblings to shop at the West Side Market. I remember my immigrant mother and first-generation father sharing their love of the old-world vibrancy of the market. I also remember how dilapidated the surrounding neighborhood was, but how it had a soul and energy that the insipid suburbs lacked.

Fast forward to the early '90s. I'm studying Urban Planning at Cleveland State University's Urban Studies College. I'd taken two study-abroad trips—to my family's farm in Ireland and later for a summer in Poland—along with more than a dozen backpacking trips to East and West Europe, Asia, South America, the Middle East, South America, and all across North America. In the process, I'd become fascinated with cities and the way the best of them can make the lives of their citizens robust and happy.

These travels inspired ideas to bring back home and have also made me love Cleveland all the more. It seems that the people who complain about Cleveland are the ones who don't have a passport.

I opened my first restaurant, Café 101, at CSU in my junior year on a whim. After an eight-year run, CSU would not renew the lease, and I was on the hunt for a new location. Thanks to my travels, I realized how lucky we are to live in Cleveland at this point in time. The opportunity in this "post-industrial frontier" is astounding, and there's no better example than Ohio City.

Wanting to control our location, my business partners and I were able to purchase the real estate for our first Ohio City venture—McNulty's Bier Markt, Bar Cento and Speakeasy—for $400,000. That's less than my Manhattan friends were paying for a closet-sized condo. The year was 2003, and people all over—from my mom to a few very, very long-term residents of the neighborhood—thought we were crazy to invest in blighted Ohio City. They thought we were completely insane in 2008, when we bought the building across the street that was condemned and a decade vacant to open Market Garden Brewery.

Then something happened. We were joined by many other like-minded entrepreneurs who opened fantastic owner-operated businesses like Crop Bistro, Soho Kitchen, Bonbon Pastry, Joy Machines Bike Shop, Johnnyville Slugger Custom Baseball Bats, Vision Yoga, and many more.

The skeptics went quiet when they saw that the rising tide actually was lifting all ships. The urban-pioneering Conway brothers of Great Lakes Brewing saw record sales at their 25-year-old brewpub. The 101-year-old West Side Market hasn't been this busy in decades. And now our biggest challenge in Ohio City is finding parking for the thousands of cars that visit each week.

Then something else happened. All of a sudden, everyone wanted in on Ohio City. The rent on my one-bedroom apartment above Third Federal Bank went up to $1,075 per month, and a years-long waiting list formed for housing in the neighborhood. Only one storefront is available north of Lorain Avenue. And nearly 2,500 residential units are under construction or shovel-ready within a ten-minute bike ride. I just bought a scruffy piece of land a three-minute walk away and will build seven fee-simple townhomes where my mortgage will be less than my current rent.

Naysayers will cry "gentrification," but progressive thinkers will see that progress and revitalization is happening at a pace and scale rarely seen.

Recognizing the need to diversify Ohio City's retail so it's not simply a restaurant/bar/brewpub district, we are actively promoting and collaborating with other forms of retail. And we're putting our money where our mouth is by purchasing the Culinary Arts Building on West 24th Street and working to convert it to a 43,000-square foot production brewery in order to distribute Market Garden Brewery beers across northeast Ohio. We'll also offer tours, tastings, and classes.

So what does the future hold for Ohio City?

Now that the commercial corridor is vibrant and largely full, the big push is on housing. As the oldest residential neighborhood in Cleveland, we've got an amazing stock of beautiful historic homes. And while most have been painstakingly restored, there are still historic restoration opportunities.

New construction — both for sale and for rent–is where we can best meet the high demand for more housing units. I, as well as other developers, am in the process of buying up buildable land within a 15-minute bike ride of the West Side Market to extend the neighborhood's energy beyond West 25th Street.

Many people are concerned about the high demand for parking in Ohio City. While it's a great problem to have, it is also a motivation to build out our neighborhood densely and vertically — and with an emphasis on public transport, protected bike lanes, and a human, walkable scale.

Sometimes people cringe when they hear words like density, walkability, bike lanes, etc. Funny, though, how we love those things in cities like Paris that were designed before the automobile became the exclusive focus of city planners. I'm struck by how people who are skeptical of bicycle commuting in the winter think nothing of skiing at sub-zero temperatures and enjoying a beer après ski ankle-deep in snow. Maybe it's time we start living the lifestyle we so admire when we holiday overseas.

Maybe that just means getting back to Cleveland's roots. Ohio City was once a dense, vibrant, walkable neighborhood with department stores, hardware shops, dentists, doctors, taverns, and breweries galore. And I hope it will be once again. We certainly are well on our way — and the best is yet to come! ◀

THE WEST SIDE MARKET

On the Cusp

HARRIETT LOGAN

The Larchmere neighborhood has been on the cusp for most of its century of existence. It's a good living, here on the perpetual precipice. Sitting on the top of an escarpment that marks the line between Cleveland and "the heights," Larchmere Boulevard is literally on a ledge, with a stellar view of Terminal Tower at sunset. The actual municipal line is a political zig-zag down the Boulevard, and it is this jagged line of mixed identity that is the bedrock of the community—one foot in the urban landscape of Cleveland, and the other in the prosperous suburb of Shaker Heights.

At the beginning of the 20th century, Woodland Avenue (now Larchmere) changed from homestead farms to a working-class Italian-Hungarian neighborhood. The development of Shaker Heights was an experimental venture, with what real estate agents would now call a diversity of housing stock: high-end condos and quintessential Cleveland doubles. Who knew this quirky architectural style would be so perfect for the current music celebration called Larchmere Porchfest?

Just a block southeast of Larchmere, the Van Sweringens built Shaker Square (1929), dubbed the second-oldest planned shopping center in the nation. The Cleveland Interurban Railroad (Shaker Rapid) began its run from downtown Cleveland to Shaker Square before construction was complete. See? Definitely a neighborhood going places. Now this neighborhood is on the Lake-to-Lake Trail, a bicycle corridor pioneering more urban-suburban transit.

While the area remained largely white until the 1970s, international headlines were made back in 1956 when Dr. Winston Richie spearheaded integration efforts in the Ludlow Community. We are home to trailblazers. And this is the kind of neighborhood that can stand up to the Federal Highway Act and win. Thanks to a women's committee from Shaker Heights who campaigned to save the "dinky little park and two-bit duck pond," Larchmere didn't become the Clark Freeway, and the Nature Center at Shaker Lakes was born. Thanks also to Mayor Carl B. Stokes, who preserved his own house on Larchmere Boulevard in the process. You want a neighborhood that speaks its mind and brings disparate groups together for a common goal? Larchmere is your mecca.

Most people describe Larchmere as a lively urban neighborhood with a quiet retail district. But how does a "quiet" urban retail district even exist in 2016? The pedestrian retail overlay zoning helps, but mostly we owe thanks to business legend John P. Sedlak, whose "street of dreams" began with 40 years on Larchmere. Nationally, mom-and-pop shops caved to franchises and fast food, and retail main streets emptied as big boxes were built further out in the 'burbs. But Larchmere was incubated in those critical years by Sedlak Interiors, encompassing 14 buildings by 1989. After Sedlak's departure for Solon, the remaining merchants banded together to keep a retail focus on art and antiques, a focus still hazily in evidence. The main drag of Larchmere was named a National Commercial Historic District in September 2015.

Larchmere is the kind of neighborhood that has no less than four community development organizations vying for jurisdiction. If this sounds less than organized, it's true. We are on the edge of greatness, but, clearly, we haven't landed. There's plenty of work to do, and there are plenty of people out there doing it. Our greatest strength can also be our greatest weakness: an independent spirit.

It took months for the local merchants association to agree on a tagline, for example, but I think the winner does the trick: Upbeat Vitality, Offbeat Charm. Festivals and events sponsored by the association highlight the homegrown ingredients that give the neighborhood a distinctive flavor: old-fashioned sidewalk sales, chess tournaments, local author book fairs, a strong hint of garlic, live music on porches, great food, artist bazaars, residential garage sales, teen basketball tournaments, antique shows, live dance and martial art demos, fashion, appraisals, targeted fundraising, mural painting, community gardening. We have a healthy appetite here.

In fact, Larchmere has won several "Best Kept Secret" awards. My Larchmere may not be your Larchmere, but that's the beauty of a good framework: there is simultaneous dichotomy and harmony. Part urban, part village, Larchmere is on the brink of being a "hot" neighborhood. Here on the threshold, we know our song is part hip-hop, part hipster, and overwhelmingly our own. Don't let the secret out; we know that being on the cusp gives us the best view of the city. ◄

Best Galleries

BY MICHAEL GILL

Editor and publisher of *CAN Journal*

Waterloo Arts This small nonprofit gallery connects to the city by reaching beyond its own walls. From provocative, bridge-building exhibits like *I Am Trans* (which focused on what it is to be transgender or transsexual), to shows like *Pretty Vacant* (which took inspiration and material from the region's glut of abandoned property), to the *Zoetic Walls* mural project (which makes the entire neighborhood a gallery), there is nothing passive or merely decorative about this place.

SPACES Having made a hard turn from the exhibition of objects to the presentation of ideas, SPACES gives artists a place to experiment. It has become the region's go-to venue for conceptual art—not things you'd find, or could fit, or maybe even want in your home, but works that will drive your conversation long into the night. And after years of planning, the organization is on the verge of a big move to the fast-developing Hingetown-branded part of Ohio City, which means it will be easy to go get a beer to keep the conversation going after your visit.

Bonfoey Founded in 1893, this is by a long shot the oldest gallery in the city. Bonfoey also represents one of the most extensive lists of artists—from significant Cleveland Schoolers of the 20th century to more than 100 contemporary artists, from the established to rising stars. At any given time you might find works of Op-Art pioneer Julian Stancsak, or contemporary lyrical abstractionist Dana Oldfather, or hyper-real portraiture by Frank Oriti. Located in the heart of downtown, indeed within a block of the Playhouse Square theaters, Bonfoey makes a great destination unto itself, or an easy stop before a show.

Zygote Press Now in its twentieth year, Zygote is the local pioneer in a trend of studios that enable artists to work in a specific medium—in this case traditional print, from intaglio techniques like etching and engraving, to relief, monoprint, silkscreening, and letterpress. The fact that other organizations have followed Zygote's lead, with facilities for paper making, analog photography, fiber, ceramics, and even woodworking, is a tribute to their success. The Zygote Gallery regularly shows the organization's connections around Cleveland and beyond, with shows by international exchange artists, concept-driven group shows, works from the archives, and occasional exhibits putting the spotlight on one or two individual artists.

HEDGE Part of a new generation of serious gallerists in Cleveland, Hilary Gent has taken up the cause of representing both rising and established artists of the region. A beautifully renovated and expansive space in the 78th Street Studios complex enables her to show large works, installations, and group shows that give each individual artist plenty of space. The 78th Street Studios' monthly Third Friday events draw huge crowds, which makes it simply a fun place to be.

Tregoning & Company Bill Tregoning has encyclopedic knowledge of Cleveland art history, and he knows how to spin a yarn—and that serves his gallery well. That's partly because in its three rooms, he commonly exhibits contemporary alongside historic works. In one room you might find the brash works of an abstract expressionist from Cleveland in the 1960s, while in another, hyper-real, contemporary drawings from Akron, or turn-of-the-twentieth-century watercolors by a Clevelander traveling in Paris. You get the idea. And it doesn't hurt that Tregoning, too, is located in the 78th Street Studios art complex, so that you can visit a multitude of other galleries at the same time.

Before It Was Hingetown

GREGGOR MATTSON

Hingetown was born as a branding exercise in 2013 on the warm corpse of Cleveland's queer scene. Anchored by the brick Striebinger block at West 29th and Detroit Shoreway, and extending down West 25th, the Near West Side once featured a gay bathhouse, half of the city's gay bars, its only gay dance club, other gay businesses, and an occasionally cruisy street scene. While some gays remain as customers and owners in Hingetown, lost are the places that were patronized by poor queers, men of color, and men looking to get off.

On the corner of the Striebinger block was A Man's World, the kind of old-school gay bar with blacked-out windows that you had to be buzzed into. The kind with extravagant decorations for every holiday and a free spread on Thanksgiving and Easter for the queers separated from their birth families, whether by choice or estrangement. The kind where some of the patrons seemed homeless, and the bouncer had facial tattoos. The kind where a Black man celebrated his first union job by buying a round of drinks for the white, Asian, and Latino strangers at the bar. The kind where the bathrooms were unisex before that was a thing, the stalls a merry-go-round of lesbians, gay men, trans women and drag queens. The kind where occasional violence trailed men to their upstairs apartments or cars. The kind with sidewalk planters that sported pansies and little American flags. The kind that was the last place you saw a good friend before he died.

Since 1995, A Man's World had been part of a complex of three gay bars that shared internal doors and a courtyard patio: The Tool Shed, ostensibly separate from A Man's World, and the basement Crossover for occasional leather/BDSM events. In their day, these three bars crowned Cleveland's Mr. Leather, and hosted dances by the Rainbow Wranglers, the gay and lesbian country/western dance group; pool league tournaments; reunions of friends and anniversaries of lovers. Hundreds of fundraisers in the bars provided a lifeline for AIDS charities, gay sports leagues, and political campaigns, but also for small discretionary funds to help people with HIV/AIDS to pay their rent, their utilities, or their funeral expenses. The Streibinger Block was the first home of what became the Cleveland LGBT Center, and hosted the first Cleveland Leather Awareness Weekend, now a multi-state charity with more than a half million in donations to its name.

Within a couple blocks along Detroit Shoreway were two other institutions. Club Cleveland at 32nd was one of the only purpose-built gay bathhouses in the United States, and the city's prime palace of promiscuity until a rival opened in 2006. Bounce on 25th was, by 2009, the only gay dance club, anchoring Cleveland's vibrant drag scene and a score of charities of its own. Down 25th past Lorain were two other racially integrated gay bars: Muggs, a working-class dive past Clark, and Argos, spitting distance from the West Side Market. Argos was a gay sports bar with a mixed audience, its reputation as African American belied by a patronage that ran at least half white. Its patio sported umbrellas, faux palms, and a view of the Ohio City skyline where gay volleyballers congregated after Sunday practice.

The Striebinger Block was also home to Burton's Soul Food and the Ohio City Café where you could grab an economical bite while you sobered up, or lay down a slick of grease to prolong the night's fun. The Dean Rufus House of Fun, alternately described as an "an upscale gay boutique," a "gay-friendly variety store," and "a gay porn shop with a large selection of soul records," was open until early morning for casual purchases of designer underwear, wigs, cock rings, poppers, or lube. On weekend mornings after last call, men streamed along Detroit, lingering for one last smoke, taking one last glance, chancing to slip their phone numbers into someone's hand, making tomorrow's plans with friends, wandering down Detroit to where Black and brown hustlers lingered, or slinking off between cars to make out...or more.

A "community building project" assumed ownership of the Streibinger block in early 2013, evicted the gay men who lived upstairs, and shuttered the bars. During the bars' last call, flyers thanked their owner, Rick Husarick, for providing "an oasis for the gay community in Cleveland; where customers, employees and tenants alike could gather together to build friendships, celebrate diversity and support the community." These goals were echoed by the new owners, who describe theirs as "inclusive," "responsible" redevelopment that will get "other people excited about doing big, sexy things in Cleveland" and satisfy their "hunger" to invest.

These continuities are nowhere to be found in journalistic accounts that invariably describe what came before Hingetown as a "decrepit," "toxic" "nowhere." Newcomers look back upon a curious frontier that was at once empty and populated, a "vacant" "no man's land" of "drug dealers and prostitutes," sidewalks "full" yet where "no one would want to walk at night."

Hingetown's queer past has grim resonance in the words newcomers use. Journalists think they're denigrating the old scene when they call it a "complex of debauchery" or a "smorgasbord of vice." Tea had long been served outside the new Cleveland Tea Revival (T, or truth, is the essential, gossipy news of queens). Men sporting leather harnesses, dog collars and leashes had long found succor in the places replaced by Harness Cycling Studio and Ohio City Dog Haven. Beats from the jukebox in A Man's World were what you could hear from the sidewalks outside what is now the Beet Jar juicebar and Jukebox city tavern. Where now stand the Mariner Lofts did occasionally loft se(a)men. And when newcomers and journalists describe the old neighborhood as shady and dingy, they inadvertently use old gay pejoratives for African Americans, who used to frequent the bars and who are most of the renters in the Lakeview public housing projects two blocks away.

Many gay men celebrate the new order. For Dean Rufus, who has outlived many neighborhood transitions, the change has been "fabulous." Getting a "more safe, upscale atmosphere" was one goal of patrons who organized a boycott of Husarick back in 2008 after a longtime AIDS activist was mugged; demands for safety accompanied complaints that the bars' troubles were caused by "lowball street rats." The newspaper *Gay People's Chronicle* (itself recently defunct) sounded the dogwhistle of racism when it telegraphed concerns over "thugs" and linked the nearby public housing to descriptions of the bars as "a bit seedy." A former Man's World bartender now helms the Urban Orchid florist in Hingetown's renovated firehouse, telling a journalist, "I don't think there's a need for a gay scene in Cleveland anymore. I go wherever I want with my friends. Every bar is a gay bar." Yet the parts of the scene that were racially and economically diverse are absent from the Transformer Station art gallery and Hingetown's other institutions.

If the Streibinger block was "a corner of poverty," it's because Cleveland queers are also poor. If we stood in the lots described by gentrifiers as "missing teeth," they reflected our own bodies. If we did not shun dealers, it's because we know that college folks get their Adderall and pot from "friends." We know all the reasons why a man on the street locks eyes with you for longer than is necessary, and why that can be so threatening if he is Black and you are white. And we know that a transgender woman is arrested for selling sex even when she's not, in a city where her safety is an afterthought.

In the great recession, Cleveland's queer oasis became a mirage: Club Cleveland closed in 2009, Argos in 2010, Muggs shortly thereafter, and Bounce, briefly, in 2015. It wasn't the recession that closed A Man's World or the nonprofit across the street that provided queer-friendly outpatient addiction treatment services. They succumbed to the recovery.

Though the American flag still flies from the corner of the Streibinger block, the gay pride rainbow flag that fluttered beneath has been replaced by the gentrifiers' standard, the Ohio City flag. Journalists eulogize the racially and economically mixed queer scenes as the "inevitable casualties" of the "community builders." These real estate entrepreneurs have succeeded in "curating" a corner of Cleveland that does not, as one publication fawned, "suck." But for us queers, not sucking is not only no fun, it's not fair. ◀

homage to...
The Velvet Tango Room

Visiting Cleveland for the first time? Have an event to celebrate? Go to the Velvet Tango Room.

Paulius Nasvytis was early to the cocktail trend when he opened this inimitable, only-in-Cleveland bar in 1996. Nasvytis's staff mix Pisco Sours and French 75s for loyal patrons, suits, local politicos, and out-of-towners who make it a destination spot. Finding it is part of the experience, as the VTR is located on a desolate stretch of a post-industrial street that is always neither here nor there.

Signs outside are off-putting, warning "no big hair" and "no golf shoes," but everything inside is inviting. Somehow the VTR manages to be pretentious and down-to-earth at once.

Nasvytis is a first-generation Lithuanian immigrant who opened the bar after working for years at Cleveland's upscale French hotel restaurant, Classics. Many nights he floats throughout the bar, dressed in a three-piece suit, sometimes presenting women with long-stemmed roses. VIPs are ushered into the hidden "members only" back room where, because everything is surprising at the VTR, busts of Lenin, Mussolini and Mao—"deposed dictators doomed to live in this capitalist hell," Paulius explains—line the shelves.

The backstory, location, and atmosphere of the VTR mix Cleveland ambitions, failures, and distinctiveness, and the drinks are no less complex and delightful. The staff make their own maraschino cherries, ginger ale, and bitters. The bartenders have ripped biceps from shaking cocktails by hand. They flambee orange slices and shake egg whites into soft peaks for Ramos Gin Fizzes. It is expensive (for Cleveland) and cheap (for what you get) at once. At the VTR, some weird alchemy makes it all work.

The Little Italy Historical Museum

MARYANN DE JULIO

With a magnifying glass, Eva M. and Lauretta N. show me where their family comes from, outside Rome, in Mille C.. We look for Campobasso on the map of Italy that's pinned to the back wall of the Little Italy Historical Museum, and then for Ripabattoni, a village in Campobasso, my grandfather's hometown.

Most of the Italians who immigrated to Cleveland's Little Italy came from the Campobasso region, just south of Rome, in the Abruzzo province. In all of Cleveland, about half of the Italians came from only ten villages of southern Italy, and nearly seventy percent from Sicily, Benevento in the Campania, and Campobasso in the Abruzzi, to rejoin old friends and relatives. I didn't know this—Lauretta laughs, says that maybe we're *paisans*, and asks if I know what that means.

Eva M. and Lauretta N. run The Little Italy Historical Museum—Lauretta's the curator. I'm here with my friend Pamela from the Western Reserve Historical Society. Pamela knows Eva and Lauretta—she likes to drop by and visit whenever she can. We're here to listen to their stories and I'm here to find a beginning for mine. Eva has set out four mugs for tea, and there are four chairs, hers at a slight distance from the others. Lauretta tells her to draw nearer.

"So you want to hear my story," Lauretta says, as she proceeds to tell us that she lives in the house that she grew up in on Random Street, that there were nine of them, nine children in the family. Random Street marks the beginning of Little Italy as you pass under the railroad trestle on Mayfield. At the intersection of Random and Mayfield is a sign for public parking. Singer Steel Company used to be where the lot is now. Lauretta tells us that as a child she would roller skate down the hill, over the blacktopped lot. Someone paved over the blacktop with cement just like the city paved over the redbrick streets, except for Murray Hill Road. The Neighborhood Association fought to keep the original surface of the Hill intact.

The Little Italy Historical Museum wasn't always where it is now, across the street from the Holy Rosary Catholic Church. For a while, it was located in the Italian Brotherhood Club—previously, a Savings and Loan for the first Italian immigrants—where Nido's Restaurant stands today. And before that, on the corner in La Dolce Vita's spot. Getting property was hard, but life could be hard—no indoor plumbing, one bath a week on Saturdays at the ALTA House that the Rockefellers built in 1895 for the community. But "Leave it to the Italians: they know how to create, to make things bloom and grow." This is what Eva says as she tells us about how she looked up one day from the ALTA House playground and every backyard in sight had a garden, a row of gardens that stretched from house to house.

Al, who's come into the Museum, says that he had a victory garden in the small plot in his front yard, but I'm not sure where because his family rented and moved all over the neighborhood before he left to join the Merchant Marine and cruise the Great Lakes from Tachawanda to Sault Ste. Marie. Two years of enjoying the scenery—the Mackinaw Islands, the twists and turns—just like being on vacation while he learned his trade as a heavy machinery operator. And Lauretta says that all you need is sunshine and water, and that she talks to the plants, especially the tomatoes, telling them to turn out okay—and they do.

"That's it," says Lauretta, a phrase she uses often to punctuate her story, meaning "that's all there is to say about that," but just as easily, "that's exactly it"—how things were or how they ought to be.

Eva and Lauretta talk about Al now. He was a rascal growing up, they say, throwing snowballs inside the theatre, setting off firecrackers. Sometimes the boys needed a little straightening out, which the men saw to. Men like Rocky Gracciano, a world-class boxer whose autographed photo is among the many that cover the museum walls. Gracciano came to Cleveland to celebrate with the young Golden Gloves Champions in Little Italy. And women like Miss Bertha J. Blue, who would call home if you didn't show up for school: *Where's Little Johnny? Where's Little Lauretta?* Everybody loved Miss Blue, whose photograph is right in front of us, in the first row, at the top.

Eva has made a packet of *chiacchieroni* newsletters for me and she offers to xerox a newspaper item about Miss Blue, who taught at Murray Hill School for forty-six years before retiring in 1947. The paper quotes from Thelma L. Pierce, whose father-in-law David Pierce was the only white president of Cleveland's NAACP. Thelma Pierce says: "The best loved first grade teacher at Murray Hill School, for 44 years was an African-American, Bertha J. Blue." Eva's own photo is in the corner of the museum that's set aside for pictures of the ALTA House: Eva, who's very petite, probably not even five feet, is seated with the other members of the girls' basketball team. She tells me that the original ALTA House burned down but that the beautiful library where she loved to go as a young girl survived. I ask if she'd mind if I wrote about her, and she says that she'd be honored. That I should read the stories in the folder she hands me, that I should take the stories in slowly, feel them. ◀

The Little Italy Historical Museum, sometimes referred to as The Little Italy Heritage Museum, closed in 2007. The Museum's archives (papers, photographs, films, objects) were donated to the Western Reserve Historical Society and are now part of their collections.

Best Museums

Thanks partially to robber barons of the late 19th century — businessmen who made a lot of money on industry and then gave back — Cleveland has a bevy of well-endowed, nationally ranked museums and cultural institutions deserving even more visitors and patronage than they already receive.

The Cleveland Orchestra Not a museum, but as treasured as one, this top-five American orchestra plays in the jewel box that is Severance Hall. Arguably the single best thing about the city.

The Cleveland Museum of Art Another nationally ranked institution, the CMA recently completed a remarkable renovation. Be sure to check out Gallery One when you enter, and have lunch in the sunny atrium.

The Rock and Roll Hall of Fame Newer to Cleveland and popular with tourists, the Rock Hall is the only place to go if you want to see your favorite guitarist's old leather jacket.

Great Lakes Science Center Go for the Polymer Funhouse, perfect for young kids on snowy days as well as a changing roster of well-curated exhibits.

The city also houses several lesser-known, equally fascinating worthy museums:

The Cleveland History Center Learn about the history of the Western Reserve — and maybe even your family — at this University Circle museum with several outposts.

The Maltz Museum of Jewish Heritage Go for both the thoughtful (Einstein) and playful (Jews in baseball) exhibits.

Cleveland Museum of Natural History The depth of the collection here is astonishing — as are the stars in the planetarium.

Polka Hall of Fame For serious Cleveland tourism.

In the Place of No Place

PEET MCCAIN

G oodrich-Kirtland Park isn't a place many Clevelanders would consider a "place." The neighborhood is one of those accounting constructs used for statistical purposes by the city, and marketing for the area is operated by the St. Clair Superior Community Development Office. But a visit to the neighborhood could be the highlight of any tourist's trip to the city. It is difficult to pinpoint exactly why it's such a great place to visit: maybe it's the lack of attention it receives by tour guides and Clevelanders alike that makes it homey and inviting.

You are unlikely to see people running around with selfie sticks in this industrial district, but here are some selfie-worthy spots to visit:

Morgan Conservatory of Paper Making grows Kozo mulberry trees that make paper, the largest grove in the U.S. The Morgan also houses the processes for turning wood into paper and the antique letterpresses for making prints and posters and other art, so you can witness the cycle from wood, to pulp, to paper and other fiber arts. Tours take less than an hour, and fill you with intellectual stimulation. Located at 1754 E. 47th Street, this is truly one of Cleveland's hidden gems.

Asian Town Center houses one of the very best and biggest Asian markets in the city. Inside Asian Town Center you can grill your own meat at the table at the excellent Miega Korean Barbeque, while Korean television plays overhead. You can shop for groceries from China, South Korea, and Vietnam at the massive Asia Food Company. **Negative Space Gallery** is a performance space/art gallery and is worth a visit if just for the wood-burning art of Gadi Zamir, the owner. It commonly hosts international artists with a wide range of styles. There are also free tai chi lessons at the mall on Sundays, and special events, such as a Chinese New Year celebration, year round.

Not generally open to the public, **Tyler Village** is an "Innovation Center," and one of the grand indicators of a return of manufacturing and commerce to the city of Cleveland. It's a repurposed industrial building that's now home to a multitude of small businesses such as Analiza, a biotech company specializing in medical analysis equipment and services, and

Digiknow, a digital marketing firm. Amenities on site include a café, dry cleaning, a gym, a conferencing facility, bicycle parking, free parking for cars, and even housekeeping services. It is also on the corridor that will contain ultra-high-speed internet connectivity. It would be fair to expect Tyler to become an attractive future home to businesses moving into the area. It also houses Gotta Groove records, one of the few places in the country that still manufactures vinyl records.

Other notable neighborhood amenites include:

Any description of **Slyman's Deli** corned beef at this point will just make the lines of people waiting for one of the best sandwiches in the U.S. longer. I don't want that so we'll stop right here. Just because it defines what corned beef in the way that croissants define Paris, doesn't mean you should go there and stand in line in front of me.

Ariel International Center: is an events space (including rooftop) that offers a spectacular view of the city, overlooking Burke Lakefront Airport, downtown, and the lake. It's currently booked for weddings eight months to a year in advance on the top two floors.

When the movers and shakers in Cleveland want dim sum, they go to **Li Wah** at Asia Plaza. Every time I've been there, I've seen politicians, or prominent theater types, or other folks in business suits with a firm hand-shake knocking back dishes like "Seafood in a Bird's Nest" or "Double Lobster with Ginger and Scallions."

Gust Gallucci's Italian Market is the quintessential Italian deli. Imports from the old country come in every day. Its variety of Italian food products is awe inducing, and Mama Gallucci is still there and will give you attitude with your Italian sub sandwich.

Every Clevelander worth their noodle soup has an opinion on The Pho Row, two excellent Vietnamese restaurants that are next door to each other

Number One Pho and **Superior Pho** near Superior and E. 31st Street. Stop by and test them both for yourself.

The **Dunham Tavern Museum** is the oldest building in Cleveland still at its original site. In 1824, Rufus and Jane Pratt Dunham opened a stage-coach stop and hosted visitors in the tavern. Through all of the many changes to happen to that section of Cleveland, this building survived and is now a museum and a lovely, rustic event space.

The city's **Mounted Police Stables** are located on 38th Street within sight of I-90. Urban farmers stop by and grab rich horse manure here for the many community gardens and farms housed in the city.

Located at 4404 Perkins Avenue, the **Studio Foundry** produces fine art statues, monuments, busts, and other projects up to 6,000 pounds at a time.

The **Masonic Auditorium** is home to the Ancient Accepted Scottish Rite-Valley of Cleveland (aka the Freemasons). This grand building at 3615 Euclid Avenue hosts many great performances in its 1920s-era venue every year. Inside, the space is splendid, with 30-foot-high ceilings atop giant marble columns. Outside, it is an enormous cube made of bricks, hiding the grandeur inside. This was a place that was built when Cleveland was on top of the world, and it is a wonder. If you go see a performance there (and you should), dressing up is the way to go.

Since their marketing is offshored to the neighborhood next door, it is difficult to find these Goodrich-Kirtland Park businesses. It is quite possible that no one in GKP wants it to be a tourist destination, or a thriving residential community. You may well be ruining their secret if you show up. I still think it is worth the visit. ◀

Best Places to Go If You Only Have One Day

Visiting town? Showing out-of-towners around? Classic itineraries would suggest you hit the **West Side Market**, **Playhouse Square** (with new, gigantic chandelier), **Lakeview Cemetery** (Tiffany stained glass!), **The Cleveland Museum of Art**, **The Cleveland Orchestra**, and pierogis at **Sokolowskis**. Along the way, you might check out **Terminal Tower**, those hulking stadia where games are played, and the gorgeous Guardians of Traffic on the **Hope Memorial Bridge**.

Over the past few years, newer must-sees have crept their way up the lists, making a play for becoming "new" classic Cleveland attractions. These include the various outdoor events sponsored by the **Cleveland Flea**, where everyone loves to see and be seen as they buy locally made items. A crowded block of great **breweries** line W. 25th Street by the West Side Market, and are popular with types who enjoy drinking late into the night. **The Happy Dog**'s two locations (west and east) offer a slew of fantastic cultural and social events, including lectures, classical music, and panel discussions, that pair nicely with their Froot Loop-topped hot dogs. New festivals with a patina of the past offer pretention-free fun, including **Dyngus Day**, **Brite Winter**, and the **Larchmere Porch Fest**. If you are taking kids around town during the winter, **The Cleveland Botanical Gardens** offers a butterfly-filled rainforest to play in, and on sunny days the newly spiffed-up **Edgewater Park** is the place to be.

Agony in the Garden:

A Lapsed Catholic's Ex-Pat's Field Guide to Our Lady of Lourdes National Shrine and Grotto

DON PIZARRO

EUCLID ▶

Parishes in the Diocese of Cleveland, and other places, have disappeared or combined, as have a number of non-diocesan Catholic high schools and religious communities. But Our Lady of Lourdes National Shrine and Grotto remains, tucked away in southern Euclid as it has been for decades, since long before I passed through grade school at St. William (now Ss. Robert and William) in the '80s. Its website says, "The Shrine is a replica of the Grotto in Lourdes, France." I couldn't tell you how close a replica since I've never been to Lourdes, France. "Incorporated into the Grotto are two stones taken from the stone upon which Our Lady appeared in Lourdes. The water from the Grotto flows over these holy relics." I was really impressed with that back in the day. Two stones from a bigger stone at the French Lourdes made this suburban Cleveland replica just as holy? Sure, why not. It was an article of faith as good as any I'd received.

If you're like me, a lapsed Catholic who prided yourself on the ability to walk into any Mass at any church after years away and still know what to say, when to stand, and when to kneel, only to lose that ability when the Mass changed during your prolonged absence, you needn't feel bad at the Shrine. Each statue of the Virgin Mary, whether in her traditional veil or in full Queen of Heaven regalia, looks upon you with the same gentle face she had when she stood on the glass-block windowsill of Sister Marian's classroom. (Everyone who's been through Catholic school remembers a Sister Marian.) And if the Shrine can offer a sense of tranquility to the pilgrim, to the sick, to the broken (according to the glass display case of testimonial letters, abandoned crutches, and discarded braces), then it can at least offer hope of the same for someone who might not otherwise go back to visit an old parish that might not hold the same meaning it once did. Or that might not even exist anymore.

As you stroll through the outdoor sanctuary, among the weathered fixtures and fittings used for the occasional Mass, seeing the awe on the faces of the statues of the children of Lourdes, you might think you hear whispers of, "You know you belong here, you've always belonged here, come home," from somewhere vaguely over your left shoulder. Ignore it. Just allow yourself to become reacquainted with the iconography and the symbolism, the meanings that the still-faithful ascribe to the Immaculate Conception and the Sacred Heart. But from a distance. It might not even be that hard. It's okay. As long as you can at least display the minimum amount of respect your old, non-Catholic schoolmates had to, like the evangelical, Muslim, and atheist kids I knew at St. Joe's (Villa Angela-St. Joseph, by the time I graduated).

This means maybe resisting the temptation to immediately Instagram the sign marked "To Stations of the Cross" posted on a stone arch, pointing to a circular walkway lined with waist-high stone markers onto which are carved each of the Mysteries of the Rosary, arranged literally like beads strung along a chain. The ones that stand out to you (for Instagramming later) may depend in large part on your state of mind at the time of your visit. When I was there with relatives after my father passed a few years ago, two lines stopped me in my tracks: "1ST SORROWFUL MYSTERY, THE AGONY IN THE GARDEN." But keep going, and once you reach the end, having walked past and read over the Joyful and Glorious Mysteries, interspersed with lifesized statues of angels, saints, and children posed as models of devotion, your feelings will probably settle into an equilibrium of sorts. Maybe not one that will send you to your knees (if it does, let it), but one you probably haven't experienced since Sister Marian's classroom.

Whether you fit the usual narrative or not—the ex-Catholic/ex-Clevelander, who once shook the parish/factory dust from your feet as you moved away to upstate New York or wherever, then came back on a boomerang return arc when you were suddenly knocked off your horse by an epiphany, this realization that you gotta be tough and you in fact have been all along, because you're from Cleveland, and Cleveland Rocks, and Alleluia what was once lost is finally found!—come to Euclid and visit Our Lady of Lourdes Shrine and Grotto. Enjoy a bit of peace and quiet in a place where the adage "You can't go home again" feels for a moment like yet another article of faith that might once have been as good as any you'd received. ◀

Best Locally Owned Stores

Big Fun Don't think toy store, think "named by *Playboy* as one the coolest stores in all of America." Big Fun has been a local favorite for 25 years, and Steve Presser's collection of new and vintage toys, retro video games, and naughty greeting cards exemplifies the independent spirit.

Cosmic Bobbins This store on Shaker Square is more than a great place to buy handmade items by over 60 artists: it is also committed to training underserved populations in sewing and arts-based entrepreneurship. Purchasing presents at Cosmic Bobbins spreads joy and does good.

Banyan Tree A Tremont staple, Banyan Tree defines Cleveland chic, featuring locally made products and stylish, contemporary items you won't find at the mall shops.

Flower Child A true mid-century department store, Flower Child offers shoppers a chance to get lost in a sea of nostalgia. The lower level is a maze of rooms packed with vintage furniture, housewares, and wearables.

Loganberry Books Larchmere's independent bookstore sells new and used books as well as a curated collection of rare and antiquarian titles. Large and inviting, it is the perfect place to spend an hour or four.

Mac's Backs Books on Coventry Three floors of new and used books, this independent bookstore is also a community hub and an incubator of young literary talent.

Music Saves Since 2004, this Waterloo store has specialized in old and new vinyl, and has an extensive indie rock inventory.

Snippets of Lee-Harvard in the 70s

JANICE A. LOWE

My old neighborhood, Lee-Harvard, now referred to as Lee-Miles, is quieter and, like the rest of Cleveland, less populated than it was in the 70s. I remember the hustle and bustle of the city then, but people look at me like I'm crazy when I refer to Cleveland's former status as a major U.S. city. I thrived growing up there before my family left when I was in tenth grade, and actively miss my native city—warts, jokes, and all. Now I am that perennial visitor trying to piece together home. Because of depopulation, wards were combined—hence the name change—and two well-loved schools, Gracemount and Beehive, were demolished. I regret that I didn't get one of the "Gracemount Bricks" distributed to commemorate its demise.

In the 70s, Lee-Harvard was a neighborhood of neatly kept bungalows and colonial-style houses with immaculate lawns and cherry and plum trees. Other than an early morning train whistle from the tracks near Miles Road, traffic and traffic noise was minimal on the side streets. We stayed in the streets, the middle of the streets, with our bike riding, touch football, and dodgeball games. My neighbors worked every job imaginable. Ford plant workers, civil servants, schoolteachers, municipal judges, and shopkeepers lived all around. Elementary schools in Lee-Harvard, like Adlai Stevenson and Gracemount, were known for their gifted programs, although that kind of tracking was controversial because of how resources were distributed, leaving some out.

My neighborhood was virtually all black during my childhood, except for a few elderly white neighbors who rarely came outside. My dad would sometimes hire an elderly white neighborhood handyman with electrician skills. My mother bought homemade Christmas cookies from Mrs. Szabo, who was Hungarian-American and the only other white person on Lee Heights who spoke to her black neighbors.

Like many of their neighborhood friends, my parents renovated their attic into bedrooms and remade their basements into gathering and home office spaces. Our family's cozy bungalow had a basement with a metal pub-type bar and a real wine cellar, with the appropriate coolness and darkness. Before we moved in, someone had planted flowers and herbs of every season so that the back, side, and front yards were mostly fragrant and in bloom.

Businesses in Lee-Harvard were often as creatively named as they were creative. The Sirrah House Night Club, for example, once had both jazz and disco in its name, I believe. Founded in the 1950s, Sirrah House is still a destination for live R&B and jazz. My Girl Scout troop held meetings there on weekends. In the era of mirror balls, black light, and sparkly fringe décor, we were excited to sit at nightclub tables and dream of jamming in ultrasparkly surroundings to The Dazz Band live, and sipping crème de menthes or whiskey sours topped by maraschino cherries.

Every time I drove past the Ju Va De Lounge (now Epic Ultra Lounge) on Harvard I wondered what the word scramble meant. Is it a rearranged spelling of De Ja Vu? A Ju Va De must've signaled some kind of rejuvenation, a rhythmic rendering of DJs and days, the good ones you have yet to experience or a par-tay with the livest bands in the future-past.

Harvard Avenue was a true thoroughfare of everything in the '70s. It had a Dearing's, founded by Cleveland's first African-American restaurateur, Ulysses Dearing, who owned several eat-in and take-out restaurants in the city. My mom bought rolls at Dearing's for special dinners. Gardell's wasn't the only candy store, but it was our closest stop for sweet or savory—for Now & Laters candy or big sour dill pickles from a jar.

Harvard also contained several important schools, founded in the 1970s as "new schools" for new times, attended by the children or grandkids of African Americans who had migrated away from Jim Crow's southern indignities. Parents were very involved. Whitney M. Young High School, now known for its gifted programs, was one of the first schools in the country to be named in honor of a civil rights leader. I remember when the building, which was the former home of Hoban Dominican, an all-girls Catholic school, re-opened as Whitney M. Young Junior High School. John F. Kennedy High School, built in the mid-1960s, was one of the first high schools to be named after the late president. The yearbook is titled "Camelot," the Mighty Fighting Eagles is the mascot, school colors are red, white, and blue, and the high-stepping team is known as The First Ladies.

Both campuses were open for all kinds of community events. I remember the ribbon cutting for the Recreation Center at Kennedy High School, and its indoor pool. The Rec Center was designed by Whitley/Whitley, an African-American-owned architectural firm with ties to the neighborhood. The neighborhood was proud of that. Later, Whitley/Whitley designed the new Lee-Harvard Branch of the Cleveland Public Library.

The Harvard Community Services Center, founded by a very civic-minded and enterprising Mrs. Rubie McCullough, regaled kids with all kinds of arts and crafts workshops. Back in the days of macramé creativity, I took a summer knitting class there and made the east side's most crooked wide belt, and then embroidered it with a phrase uttered by Snoopy, in awful blue and orange yarn.

On Saturdays during the school year, a short, periwinkle blue bus would pick kids up in front of the Dairy Queen on Harvard and ferry us to a roller skating rink like the Blue Goose or Seven Bells—both outside of Lee-Harvard but popular destinations for the younger set. My small self would skate to the carpeted middle pole and just hang on while trying not to fall. It wasn't easy keeping out of the way of whizzing teens boogying, bouncing, and rolling backwards and forwards to the latest sounds.

I studied music after school at St. Henry Catholic Parish, The Cleveland Music Settlement's Lee-Harvard outpost. You took theory class theory for a semester, I believe, before studying an instrument. I chose piano and later, flute. My family's purchase of a piano was a big deal; a few of my friends came over to the house to practice until their families bought one. I'm sure my mother found ours at an estate sale; she had friends who were experts at hunting for and scoring valuable and often antique furnishings at decent prices, and they shared shopping tips.

On the grounds of St. Henry, Bee-Buzz Baseball, the local Little League outfit, ran a large-scale youth league. I remember watching my brother and our schoolmates in many a summertime game. Until he was deemed near-sighted and fitted with glasses, my brother struck out way too often. It was painful to watch but I was loyal. Mr. Fontana was serious about coaching, too. I know of at least one neighborhood kid, Craig Thompson, who made the pros as an outfielder for the LA Dodgers. His mother taught some of those crafts classes at Harvard Community Services Center.

Paul Warfield, formerly of the Cleveland Browns, and later a running back for the Miami Dolphins, once lived on Harvard and owned a Firestone franchise on Lee.

From the Lee Road businesses, you could buy and dress a car, deck out various ages of humans in the latest fashions, buy your favorite albums, stock up on black light posters or incense, and get your southern-style fried shrimp or whiting. On Lee, you could get your boogie on or go out for an evening of jazz.

You could also go to the Shaker Theater, which, despite its name, was technically in Cleveland, in Scottsdale, on the border with Shaker Heights. Shaker Heights was known for its tony Tudor dwellings and highly regarded school system; the Shaker Theater was known as the Palace of Blaxplotaiton Films. I remember hearing radio spots (WJMO) and seeing magazines (*JET*) advertising *Superfly*, *Blackula*, and *The Mack*. I so wanted to see these films but I was never allowed. We'd go for a family outing to see a very tame *Uptown Saturday Night* or the like.

At the juncture of Lee and Harvard was The Lee-Harvard Shopping Center. The local outpost of Hough Bakery was the go-to shop for perfectly iced birthday cakes and hot cross buns at Easter. In December, school choirs sang carols on outdoor risers. Snow and ice didn't stop anything. Hough Bakery is no more but their recipes live forever online.

Near the shopping center was the old Lee-Harvard Branch of the Cleveland Public Library. Seeing films there like *The Red Balloon* and a documentary featuring a young Roberta Flack fired up my imagination. It's where I outdid myself borrowing and reading dozens of books, some beyond my understanding.

Black-owned businesses and civic-minded black neighborhood folk anchored the area. Everyone was interested in bringing in jobs, organizing activities for kids, keeping crime down, and nudging neighbors to keep their lawns looking good.

Residents of Judson Drive outdid each other twice a year with ritzy and colorful house displays of Easter egg decorations and Christmastime wonderlands. The neighborhood creativity brought sightseers from all over, asking, "Can we go see the lights on Judson?" It was better than Higbee's.

My dad was active in and held office in the Lee-Harvard Community Association, which held meetings in the basement of Lee Road Baptist Church. Representatives of block associations or street clubs met, aired grievances related to the city's infrastructure, planned community clean-ups, organized meetings with public school officials, planned the annual Back to School Parade and fundraising raffle, raised college scholarship money, brought in jobs for youth … the list goes on. LHCA was big on organizing discussions between elected officials and residents. It was said that no one could run for office without participating in the Lee-Harvard's infamous candidates' forums. Our congressman was Louis Stokes, founder of the Congressional Black Caucus. He was very visible in Cleveland and would show up at community events when the neighborhood honchos called on him to address community concerns.

I lived on Lee Heights Blvd., very close to Harvard. Our street club was super organized. My former neighbors helped me call up some Lee Heights street club lore. Anthony, who had the cool bike with the steering wheel, laughed about his sister's obsession with the club's long-ago trips to Euclid Beach, and the way her eyes would well up with tears from either happiness or wind as she rode The Flying Turns. Stacey from down the street recalls a street club trip to King's Island all the way in Cincinnati in later days.

What we all remember best was prep for the Lee-Harvard Day—our back-to-school parade, our end of summer ritual theater. The street clubs were the parade. Clubs elected queens. Queens rode in the parade in carts decorated by neighborhood kids and pulled by a family car. Everyone re-members going over to the Glenns' to decorate the cart the year their daughter Linda and Stephanie Jones were street club royalty. Linda's brother Kevin reminded us of his dad's dark green convertible Skylark pulling the cart, the chariot floating down the street with style. There was also the year that street club president Mr. Long let us deck out his camper like a yellow school bus.

Yes, bands played, high steppers stepped, and politicians did the ex-pected walk and wave, but if you had a person in a cart, you would walk next to it or escort the cart with your bike as Kevin and Walter did the summer their sisters reigned. One year, dressed in white on white with white visors, my brother and I, along with my dad and Mr. Hyche, both officers in LHCA, "walked" at the head of the parade. Nine and ten years old, we scampered up Glendale waving and smiling like we were running for mayor.

Queens competed by selling raffle tickets, a fundraiser for the LHCA. Later in the day, the drawing would happen at a program with community leaders, politicians, and the people who elected them in attendance. Prizes were donated by local businesses. The winning queen would be crowned with a tiara. Street clubs were the stars supreme.

The block, of course, hosted an end of summer block party and barbecue, but Stacey reminded me of the Halloween parties the street club organized after news reports circulated of tampered-with treats finding their way into Cleveland candy bags. Neighbors alternated volunteering their basements as the party spot, complete with bobbing for apples and Mrs. Ragland's better-get-yours-before-they're-gone popcorn balls.

The barricades on Invermere, the border of Shaker and Lee Harvard—I remember when they were small enough to step over or walk a bike through. Over the years, they became more barrierlike. Erected to control traffic, it felt other than that, as if someone felt Clevelanders needed to work harder to pass through to Shaker. I just wanted to see my friends. I lived a couple of blocks from Shaker and had friends all over the 'burbs. The barriers were definitely a nuisance.

As a visitor, I have seen and enjoyed some of Cleveland's renaissance but still find it unsettling that Lee-Harvard is quieter than ever. That must be the New York in me. Some years ago, I had a chance to compare when I taught a two-week residency in poetry and printmaking at Gracemount School. The kids were delightfully engaged but looked at me like I was a crazy dinosaur when I asked them to "make some noise."

I wonder if that patch of woods behind Whitney Young is still there. I wonder if the courts at Kerruish Park—where we played in the National Junior Tennis League and competed with kids from all over the city—are still operational.

The rabbits who enjoyed our flower beds must have come from those Whitney Young woods. They obviously loved the quiet of Lee-Harvard, their flower bedroom community. ◀

Unexpectedly Great Reasons to Live in Cleveland

Bicycling Sure, potholes and the occasional angry driver can be a bit of a hindrance, but overall, biking lives large. We've got the only velodrome in Ohio, a constant increase in bike lanes along with links to existing Cleveland Metroparks paths, the Towpath Trail, and Cuyahoga Valley National Park.

Cuyahoga County's Community Partnership for Arts and Culture (CPAC)/ Cuyahoga Arts & Culture (CAC) What started with voters approving a tax on cigarettes to support arts and culture has turned into a powerhouse of community, investing more than $15 million annually and providing resources to arts and cultural endeavors. Their support of thousands of experiences impacts those in and around the county more than most realize.

Rowing Cleveland now has two boathouses in the Flats which house six high school, three college, and one adult team — more than 1,500 rowers total. Each September, our crooked river is also the site of the Head of the Cuyahoga — one of the largest one-day rowing regattas in the country.

Beaches Maybe it's not the ocean, but when you are enjoying some sunshine on the hot sand, looking across Lake Erie toward Canada, your mind and body won't know the difference. Along with the sand and sun, Cleveland beaches boast easy access, plenty of space, activities, great people watching, events, and memorable sunsets.

Gay Community A tight-knit and growing LGBT community calls Cleveland home. Cleveland got to showcase their hospitality in 2014 when it hosted the Gay Games and has gay-friendly bars, restaurants, and events aplenty.

Lottery League This self-described "Part rock n' roll circus, part game show, part city-wide art project" started in Cleveland in 2007. It is a triennial event where musicians are "drafted" onto teams that then collaborate as a new band and create original music. Experimental artistic unification at its best.

What's In a Name?

TOM ORANGE

BROOKLYN CENTRE ▶

W hat's in a name? In my neighborhood, confusion. Countless lifelong Greater Clevelanders have asked me, "So what part of town do you live in?" and I always begin my answer, "Well, the city calls it 'Brooklyn Centre,' but..." Before I can finish, my questioner inevitably pipes up, "Oh, you mean Old Brooklyn?" No, if I meant Old Brooklyn, I would have said Old Brooklyn. "Oh, you mean Brooklyn the suburb?" No, not Brooklyn the suburb, and not the suburb of Brooklyn Heights either. If my questioner gives me a chance, I will usually try out "Archwood-Denison" for a response, and if that meets with a blank stare, I'll usually say, "it's near the zoo." Final answer.

Here's the quick history lesson. At some point 200 years or so ago, everything west of the Cuyahoga River in the Connecticut Western Reserve was called Brooklyn Township. Two villages developed in the township: one village near the lake, around the intersection of Pearl and Detroit Roads, eventually incorporated as the city of Ohio and then, like nearly everything else in area, was annexed into Cleveland, yet retained some identity as the neighborhood of Ohio City; another village farther to the south, around the intersection of Pearl and Denison Roads, never incorporated, was annexed into Cleveland and eschewed identity for the confusion with various other Brooklyns that still exists today.

Add to the name confusion the infrastructural obstruction known as I-71, which plows right through the west-east axis of Brooklyn Centre from Fulton Road to West 25th Street/Pearl Road, and the result is a neighborhood with some challenges. Highways really do not help a neighborhood cohere, grow or flourish, but they do encourage easy flight. Which is important, because otherwise there aren't a lot of so-called modern conveniences here: we lost our one grocery store a few years ago, and our one shopping center can barely keep a furniture rental store and a check-cashing place open. We have three fast food joints, a lot of corner stores, a lot of bars, and a lot of churches.

Paradoxically though, Brooklyn Centre is all about location, location, location: with I-71's first southbound exit out of downtown running right through the neighborhood, you have quick and easy car access to almost every other part of town. You also have access to four or five major bus lines, and bike access has improved a great deal too since Fulton, Denison and West 25th have all been repaved within the past year. (If you like to bike the C&O Towpath, that trailhead below the Harvard-Denison Bridge is very close too.)

Beyond easy flight elsewhere, Brooklyn Centre's greatest asset is its mixed stock of affordable and attractive housing. Unlike some near west-side neighborhoods with long, skinny streets containing row after row of shoddily built worker shacks that were never well cared for, Archwood Avenue in particular (one block north of Denison) has some beautiful century homes, generally closer to West 25th than Fulton. Those early village settlers built well, and you can see where the original homesteaders set up shop, with more affordable single and two-family homes filling in between. The other avenues north of Archwood (Mapledale, Riverside, and then in the sliver of the neighborhood north of I-71, Poe and Library) also have some nice houses. Some of these are going to be beyond typical starter-home budgets, but they're still going to be a lot cheaper than the trendier near west side neighborhoods. You can find decent old colonials that don't need extensive rehabbing in the low five figures. And if you're in the market for a 19th-century historic church, one of those sold in my neighborhood a few years ago for the middle five figures.

Vestiges of history and culture survive here. Like Ohio City and Tremont, Brooklyn Centre hosts one of Cleveland's century-old Carnegie-funded neighborhood branches of the Cleveland Public Library, where I do most of my internet work and procure the latest reads and video entertainment. Riverside Cemetery, perched on the outer bank of I-71's Metro curve, is peaceful, if not quite as illustrious as Lakeview Cemetery. Art House, on Denison, is a non-profit arts facility that offers workshops and a monthly family-oriented open house in addition to facilitating arts instruction at the local public schools. (Not being a parent, I can't add anything about neighborhood schools.) Moncho's, a Colombian-owned cafe, just opened up this year and offers daily specials, small plates and Wi-Fi—the closest thing we have to coffee shop culture.

Beyond that, there are plenty of neighborhood bars, The Ugly Broad being my favorite. Sherry Perry has been running the place since 1981, and I'm pretty sure the bar's name preceded her. With a pool table, dozens of

John Wayne photos on the wall, bad 1970s rock and current pop-country faves on the jukebox, a bookshelf with some old paperbacks and a few board games, and Sherry's dog Shiloh snoozing in her bed near the entrance, it's the kind of place you walk into with a few friends, everyone puts a $10 bill on the bar, and you buy each other rounds all night. No live music, not big enough for that. A functioning kitchen that serves one entree per night that vegetarians will need to skip, and then various clambakes and rib cook-offs throughout the year. It's a real "family" bar. I'll never forget when I first walked in there, behind the bar a sign was posted: This Saturday, $10 all-you-can eat spaghetti dinner, to benefit Donna's son Mike. Clearly I was not the target audience, not knowing Donna or what kinda shit Mike got into, but I felt welcome all the same. These are folks looking out for each other.

Twice a year, the neighborhood gets together for the Archwood Street Fair, held the first weekend in June and September, where all the neighbors come together to put their unwanted crap out on their front lawns to sell. Sometimes you can find a real bargain, but mostly it's worth people-watching, putting neighbors' faces to houses, and the home-cooking that folks sell from their front lawns: Polish Boys, barbequed chicken, tamales, pupusas, cod fritters, you name it. It's the neighborhood at its best, all different kinds of folks coming together to acknowledge that, hey, we may not have it great here, but we don't have it all that bad either. I mean, sure we've got crime, boarded up vacant houses and absentee landlords, but we've also got some former vacant lots that folks have turned into community gardens, and I met a couple that started a fruit tree orchard along the ridge of Big Creek Valley a few years ago.

I know some neighborhood activists who feel strongly that Brooklyn Centre is poised to become hip and trendy, the next Tremont or Gordon Square. But honestly, does Cleveland really need or want that? *Cleveland Scene* said it best about a dive bar here: this is the kind of bar that hipsters would flock to, if hipsters lived in this neighborhood, which they don't, and that's exactly the way the locals like it. Let celebrity chefs, developers, and the monthly art-walkers colonize Gordon Square, Collinwood and Slavic Village. We'll visit from time to time, and then take that short drive back to our un-hip, un-trendy Brooklyn Centre home. ◀

Best Dive Bars

Usually cheap, probably dingy, and certainly a dose of the true flavor of the town.

Pats in the Flats Down the hill from bustling Tremont, near the West 3rd Street Bridge, Pats is all dive. Looking at the exterior you could think it's abandoned (hell, the upstairs windows are boarded up). Once inside though, you know you are in the right place. Beers, bands (the White Stripes played their first show outside Detroit here), and the kind of staff and clientele that are the definition of dive.

Parnell's Pub On Lee Road and a nice place to grab a beer before or after a film at Cedar Lee. But you don't need a movie as an excuse to come here. Belly up to the bar and soak in the atmosphere. Beer, dart boards, friendly bartenders … just what the doctor ordered.

S S & W Boardwalk Just a few doors down from the Beachland Ballroom, so the crowd tends to pick up before and after shows, but during non-show times, it's your standard dive in a rising neighborhood.

Carney's Top O' the Flats On the west bank of the Flats, your standard issue bar. Not as grungy as some dives, but it qualifies. No frills, mostly blue collar, cheap drinks, plus a bar dog named Billy. Bonus: a patio in the event you want some fresh air.

Rowley Inn This gem is tucked in the back streets of Tremont, right across from the Christmas Story House. Bar bowling, cheap drinks, quality food, a hearty jukebox.

Mars Bar Dark, cozy in a dive sort of way, with a good selection of drinks and surprisingly delicious gyros.

B and G Tavern B&G doesn't open until 9:30pm, but that works for its regulars. Cheap eats, cheap drinks, pool tables, and the gentle glow of a Spuds MacKenzie decorating one end of the bar keeps the mood just right.

Ontario Street Café Despite being on busy Ontario Street, directly across from the Jack Cleveland Casino, this bar is easy to miss, but if you want a dive downtown this is your place. Dim lighting, amazingly cheap booze, Genesee beer on tap, tasty sandwiches, a solid R&B/soul-anchored jukebox, and a refreshingly diverse crowd.

Union House Bar & Restaurant This classic spot has something for everyone. Bands, sports on the TV, fish fry, food deals (wings and mussels!), and of course, cheap drinks.

League Park

VINCE GUERRIERI

On April 21, 1910, League Park opened at the corner of East 66th and Lexington Avenue. The ballpark, a two-deck grandstand accommodating 21,000 fans, replaced a wooden single-level structure that opened for the Cleveland Spiders of the National League in 1891. The new League Park was state of the art, as the first stadium construction boom was well underway. The new stadiums were billed as fireproof, with steel and concrete allowing for multiple decks.

In its brief existence, League Park II hosted a World Series champion, a Negro League champion and an NFL champion. But by the 1960s, it was nothing but a memory, as the neighborhood around it became the symbol for racial and economic unrest for Cleveland and the United States.

The original League Park was also at East 66th and Lexington. As baseball was starting to take hold, and permanent homes were being built for baseball teams—in the days before public funding of stadiums—one overriding consideration determined where they would be built: Could the team owner get the land cheap?

As it turned out, Frank Robison could. He and his father-in-law Charles Hathaway built streetcars and operated railways in the city, and were able to build the ballpark at the end of a streetcar line in Hough, a neighborhood that had been annexed into the city in 1872 and had become a haven for the well-to-do by the time the first League Park opened in 1891.

Hough included the city's "Millionaires' Row," Euclid Avenue, called one of the finest streets in America by Mark Twain. Industrialists built palatial mansions close enough to the factories that sprouted up as the population of Cleveland swelled, but far enough away to offer space for huge homes and pastoral lawns. Elite private schools, like University School, also came to the neighborhood, and Baker Electric, a company manufacturing electric cars for the wealthy (Thomas Edison had one, and there was one in the White House garage), made sure to put a showroom on Euclid Avenue at East 71st Street.

But by the time the second League Park was built in 1910, those captains of industry were starting to move farther east, to University Heights and Cleveland Heights, in part because the pollution their factories generated was starting to creep into their neighborhoods, and with auto travel, they could afford to commute.

The Indians won their first pennant in 1920 and defeated the Brooklyn Dodgers in what was then a best-of-nine World Series. The neighborhood around League Park had become an ethnic working- and middle-class enclave. Mansions gave way to smaller single-family homes and apartment buildings — some of which accommodated the Indians players.

In 1928, Cleveland voters approved a bond issue for a new multi-purpose stadium on the shores of Lake Erie (contrary to popular belief, NOT in an effort to get the 1932 Olympics; the only Olympics applied for by Cleveland were in 1912 and 1916), and on July 1, 1931, Cleveland Municipal Stadium opened with Max Schmeling defending his heavyweight championship with a 15th-round technical knockout of Young Stribling.

League Park's days were numbered.

The Indians played their first game at Municipal Stadium on July 31, 1932, against the defending American League champion Philadelphia Athletics. Nearly 79,000 people came out to see Lefty Grove shut out the Indians in a 1-0 pitchers' duel. Mel Harder took the loss. By comparison, the day before, 5,000 fans came out to see the game at League Park.

But in the depths of the Great Depression, the Indians weren't able to fill Municipal Stadium, and soon made League Park their permanent home again. The Tribe would play Sunday and holiday games, and, as night baseball became more popular, night games at Municipal Stadium.

In the 1940s, League Park also served as home to the Cleveland Buckeyes, a Negro League team. The Buckeyes won the Negro World Series in 1945, and played in another in 1947.

League Park also served as a football venue, as the home field for the Cleveland Rams, who won an NFL title in 1945, playing home games at League Park but the NFL Championship at Municipal Stadium. The Rams then decamped to Los Angeles, ceding the city to a new team, named for its coach, in a new league: The Cleveland Browns.

After the 1946 baseball season, Bill Veeck bought the Indians. Every game played at League Park reflected money left on the table to him, and the Indians made Cleveland Stadium their full-time home. The only regular tenants left were the Cleveland Buckeyes, but integration of Major League Baseball, while a sign of progress, spelled the end of the Negro Leagues.

By the early 1950s, League Park was gone. The city had taken possession of the property and tore down most of the stadium in 1951, leaving behind part of the grandstand wall along East 66th, and a building at the corner of East 66th and Lexington that had served as ticket offices for the Indians.

The neighborhood around it changed as well. Hough went from being 5 percent nonwhite in 1950 to more than 74 percent nonwhite a decade later—a consequence of suburbanization, with some white flight and blockbusting thrown in. In 1966, Hough burned, as riots did millions of dollars in property damage and killed four people before the National Guard was called in. Anyone who had the wherewithal fled the neighborhood at that point.

Fannie Lewis represented Hough for almost 30 years on Cleveland City Council, from 1979 to her death in 2008. In that time, she advocated tirelessly for a rehabilitation of League Park as a community center. It happened six years after she died, but it finally happened.

The ballpark reopened to great fanfare in August 2014. The old building is now home to the Baseball Heritage Museum, and the field—with the same dimensions and configuration as when the Indians played there, but covered in artificial turf—is available for rental by the city.

The Indians still play downtown, but since 1994, it's been at Progressive (née Jacobs) Field, which was the vanguard of the new trend in stadiums: A baseball-only park with state-of-the art amenities, including revenue-generating luxury boxes and club seats, while hearkening back to classic stadiums … like League Park. ◄

THE DOG POUND

Slavic Village:
A Guide

MICHAEL BROIDA

SLAVIC VILLAGE ▶

To visit Slavic Village, preferably wait until a bitterly cold evening in February, and in the dark and the snow, take the I-77 North exit for Pershing Avenue. Turn west, and as the road becomes a dead-end, ignore the sparseness of the streetlights and the horrifying industrial shapes rearing up from the barbed-wire fences on either side of you. Ignore the stark and abstract loneliness of the place, how if you were going to be murdered this would be a great, really clichéd place to be murdered in a horror-movie kind of way. At the end of the road, be sure to kill the engine and the lights to take it all in. Remember that some old timer at a Polish deli told you that this used to be a bridge that spanned the river valley all the way to Tremont, but now Pershing Avenue just peters out into the infinity of the evening, chunks of rebar and concrete hanging out over the broad expanse of the valley like something out of a Philip Levine poem. The only thing between you and an accidental, doom-filled tumble is a chain-linked fence.

Yet above you is the blast forge of the steel mill, and from its vast mouth roars the brightest, most terrifying fire you've ever seen: bigger than a skyscraper and singular in the night sky. This is what you've come to see, a religious moments of sorts. You wonder if this is what Moses felt when seeing the burning bush, the kind of unrestrained and simultaneous biblical awe and puny, insignificant smallness, that what you're witnessing in that nighttime burn is a power greater than that of men, that you're seeing the pure execution of industry and the culmination of generations of thought and ingenuity. You realize, in a come-to-Jesus moment about this place, that all the ramshackle little duplexes, all the tired-looking storefronts, all the empty lots and blownout brick warehouses are tied to this flame, that this power goes beyond blast forges and rolling presses, beyond economics and payrolls, that the spirit of the very city is tied deeply to that flame, and here you are, on its altar. Industry, the steel, slag, and creosote, are the bones of this place, even from the bright, crowded restaurant lights of East 4th Street to the County Line atop Mayfield Hill. When you have felt the scales fall from your eyes, be sure not to tarry too long. When you leave, be sure to tell all you meet: the Rust Belt lives. In fact, it burns brightly. ◀

Best Neighborhood Restaurants

Eating well in Cleveland is both easy and convenient. Below are some favorites sent in by our neighborhood essay writers.

Prosperity Social Club In Tremont, this mish-mash of dive bar, great food, and mini-bowling is a local favorite.

Slovenian Workman's Home Fish Fry Waterloo's Slovenian Home (not to be confused with other fine Slovenian Homes around town) is said to be the best, served by the "Kitchen Angels" every Friday.

Hot Sauce Williams With outposts around the city, this long-standing locally owned joint serves some of the best ribs in town.

Sterle's Slovenian Country House Don't just go for the hearty food—go also for the live polka and to watch three-generation families sprawling down the long tables.

Szechuan Gourmet Asiatown offers a number of great Chinese restaurants, including this one, where it is always best to order off the pictures hung on the wall instead of the menu. **Wonton Gourmet**, **Superior Pho**, and **Map of Thailand** are runner-up picks in this competitive category.

Villa Y Zapata The place on the west side for both chile rellenos and fanciful exterior paint jobs.

Mama Santa's There is no shortage of debates over which is the best restaurant in Little Italy, but Mama Santa's wins for its no-nonsense décor and classic 1950s red sauce cuisine.

The Isolation of The Flats

SANDY GRIFFITH

Piles.

Piles of limestone, piles of gravel, piles of broken glass. Items haphazardly piled as if to signal that no one cares what happens here. Prime views of Terminal Tower, the tallest building in the world outside New York City until 1953, obstructed by barbed wire and industrial waste. Empty parking lots advertising ridiculously low monthly rates. Space is clearly not a limiting factor in the Flats.

Beginning with Moses Cleaveland's arrival in the 18th century, the area around the banks of the Cuyahoga River benefited from Cleveland's role as a key shipping site and saw considerable industrial development mixed with periodic collapse and decline. By 1969, the year of the Cuyahoga River's most infamous pollution-driven fires, the surrounding Flats had fallen into persistent decay and abandonment. This all changed in the '80s and '90s when nightclubs, shops, and music venues turned the area into a lively entertainment district. After a brief period of prosperity, a series of drowning deaths in the summer of 2000 occurred along with an increase in crime and safety concerns. Most visitors were scared away.

Businesses shuttered and the Flats once again went dark.

Aside from a few pockets of revitalization, the bulk of the area remains desolate today, despite its strategic location between downtown Cleveland and the in-demand neighborhoods of Tremont and Ohio City. Many Clevelanders I meet don't seem to give the Flats a second thought or they avoid them entirely, but not me. I haven't lived in Cleveland very long. Unlike many other young people moving to Cleveland, I'm no boomerang. I didn't grow up here, leave to explore the world, then return. I arrived almost two years ago from Philadelphia, fresh out of graduate school and excited for a challenging new job, optimistic about the Rust Belt revitalization I'd read about in the latest trend piece heralding Cleveland as the new Brooklyn. While I do encounter many signs of this revitalization, the city still doesn't feel right to me. A mismatch. Except one place: the Flats.

I'm drawn to them, over and over: unhurried walks on the rare clear winter's day; standing below the brittle skeleton of a discarded bridge, soon to disappear from the world; late-night bike rides past seemingly abandoned buildings with suspicious and solitary lights shining inside.

Maybe it's the risk. Maybe it's the fear. I came from a city with its share of crime (during the summer, shooting rates would often climb, turning Philadelphia into "Killadelphia") where late-night walks home came requisite with my car(e)-free lifestyle. In response, I developed an internal safety meter, largely calibrated by the level of isolation on a given block. Fast-forward to Cleveland, where the city is built for twice as many people as currently live here, leaving wide swaths empty and poised to set off my safety alarm at all times of the day. There are only two directions this can lead: concluding that I am indeed unsafe and should avoid going places alone; or, realizing on an intellectual level that my internal meter may be miscalibrated, but left with a sinking sense of dread I cannot shake.

Perhaps the attraction is also an alignment of the solitude I feel in a city that's not mine with a place that's truly isolated. Because frankly, much of Cleveland feels this way to me but is less obviously desolate. Standing on empty downtown streets, the desertion leaves me with a feeling that something is off—a dissonance between what I expect and the reality of what is present. I look for evidence of the famed "Millionaires' Row" on Euclid Avenue and find only overgrown lots where mansions once were, yet the occasional business or passerby allows me to maintain at least the illusion of occupancy. But there is nothing to mask this emptiness in the Flats, thereby reducing the dissonance between the identity of the place and the feeling it inspires.

This past fall, I went to my first Ingenuity Fest, a cultural staple in Cleveland for the last decade, self-described as a festival of art and technology. Walking into the repurposed warehouse space amidst downtown lakefront docks, I was immediately reminded of the annual Fringe Festival in Philadelphia that I had attended religiously before moving to Cleveland. For two weeks every September I would gorge myself on experimental performance art of all kinds, much of it amazing, some cringe-worthy, but all exciting. Although the performances were the focus, the nightly festival bar—housed in a warehouse overflowing with performers, attendees, onlookers (really, anyone worth meeting), cheap drinks, and a dance floor—formed the fabric that glued the geographically and thematically diverse pieces together into a cohesive event. I hold many prized memories of nights at the festival bar, my clothes sticky from the humidity of the still-present summer mixed with the densely packed dance floor, and filled with the magical sense that anything was possible. These nights were my personal version of the experimental performance art I saw at the festival —equally likely to turn amazing or cringe-worthy, but always exciting.

Given the space's similar feel to the Fringe Festival, I had understandably high hopes for Ingenuity Fest. The exhibits were indeed the exciting and experimental showcase everyone had told me about. Yet while I was there—perhaps it was the rainy weather that particular night—it felt as if someone assembled all the cool pieces, but no one came. At an outdoor dance floor, sandwiched between Lake Erie and the downtown skyline, I could almost see the throngs of bodies, sweaty and electric, but they were mostly shadows in my mind. The DJ, feeling it too, said "Yo, I'm glad you're having such a good time—all seven of you." I wandered around for a bit, then left on my own, unaccompanied by any sense of magic or possibility.

Biking home alone through the Flats that night, I was caught in a downpour wearing only a sleeveless dress, clinging to September's last gasps of summer—but it was not a summer rain. The wet chill could not conceal the coming winter. I didn't know it at the time, but it would start snowing in mid-October and Cleveland would experience one of its harshest winters on record. Yet that rainy September night, I stopped on the Carter Road Bridge overlooking the lit-up downtown skyscape, a powerful symbol of urbanness seated directly adjacent to the ghost town in which I stood, and felt suddenly at ease. Finally, the dissonance had disappeared, leaving me alone with the Flats: a person and a space, both out of place. ◀

Best Hikes

BY MATT STANSBERRY

Belt Magazine columnist and author of *Red Horse: A Rust Belt Bestiary*

Sylvan Loop/Overlook Trail, North Chagrin Reservation: This short hike winds through a forest of 400-year-old beech trees and massive oaks. The A.B. Williams Memorial Woods, named after Cleveland Metroparks' first naturalist, are part of the remnant 1% of old growth forest left east of the Mississippi River. Wildflowers blanket the forest floor in spring.

Cleveland Lakefront Nature Preserve: Managed by the Port of Cleveland, this site formerly known as Dike 14 is a birding hot spot. The manmade 88-acre peninsula juts out into Lake Erie and was actually formed from sediment dredged from the Cuyahoga River. You can see the Cleveland Browns' Stadium from the overlook on the west side, but you would probably have more fun looking for deer, coyotes, and wild turkeys.

Wendy Park: Wendy Park is a 22-acre woodlot on Whiskey Island in the heart of downtown. It's part of Cleveland Metroparks Lakefront Reservation. Somehow this tiny green patch in the heart of the city hosts thousands upon thousands of birds each year, and other migrants crossing Lake Erie, from bats to monarchs. Wander down to the mouth of the Cuyahoga and see what the locals are reeling up from the water.

Ledges Trail and Beaver Marsh, CVNP: There are over 125 miles of trails in the Cuyahoga Valley National Park, but if you had to pick the best ones:

The Ledges Trail is a 2.2-mile loop with sheer sandstone cliffs rising out of a hemlock forest. The rock formations are stunning, and the southeast corner overlooks the Cuyahoga Valley. Be there at sunset in the early fall.

Beaver Marsh: The Towpath Trail along the Ohio & Erie Canal is an 85-mile marvel, built between 1825 and 1832 so mules could tow canal boats full of goods and people, connecting the Great Lakes to the Mississippi. Get incredibly close to great blue Herons, red-winged blackbirds, tree swallows, snapping turtles, water snakes, and dragonflies.

Neighborhood Lessons in Diversity

PHYLLIS BENJAMIN

The train left NYC bound for Cleveland in the winter of 1944. Soldiers gave their seats to Rachel, my mother, and me, a five-and–a-half-year old. Samuel, my father, and Burton, my teenage brother, sat with the soldiers on the floor in the aisles. I clutched my Aunt Jemima doll and Uncle Remus book, gifts from Brooklyn relatives who wished us well in our new Cleveland home. These odd-seeming gifts previewed my new life in a multicultural Mount Pleasant neighborhood, south of the downtown luxuries of Halle's Department Store and the Palace Movie Theater.

Kinsman Road is the main Mount Pleasant thoroughfare. Residents living here in the 1940s were Germans, Czechs, Russians, Jews, and Italians. Mount Pleasant took pride in the fact that blacks were among its earlier citizens. Being white and Jewish, I learned about diversity there.

During the war, apartments were scarce, but we rented a large two-bedroom apartment at 3416 East 139th Street, off Kinsman Road. Mother lied to Mr. Epstein, our landlord, who only would rent to a family with one child. She then charmed him with her beauty so I could come out of hiding and be seen.

I entered the second semester of kindergarten at Robert Fulton Elementary School, a sturdy, well-designed building with glass block hallway floors. A picture of my fourth-grade verifies that about seven "Negroes" were in my class. (I have this picture.) I soon became best friends with Laverne. In first grade I asked my mother if I could give her one of my dolls, telling her that Laverne was "colored." My mother said her skin color didn't matter and of course I could give her this prized gift.

For six years the school focused on children in cultures around the world. I loved my friends, the principal, and teachers who gave me confidence to be a class leader. I was one of four students chosen to spend the entire fifth grade year on the road being filmed for teacher-training movies. In my yellow sweater, embroidered with strawberries, and a short red skirt, I was photographed all over town. I remember the steaming fiery vat of the furnace burning molten iron at Republic Steel.

As a young teen, coincidently, I worked as a secretary for my father, who managed a steel company. After I asked him if I could one day sell steel, he advised that I could only hope to become an English teacher because I was a woman.

Speaking of furnaces, my job was to shovel coal from our apartment basement bin into our furnace section. Cranking the clothes wringer on the machine and hanging wash on the lines were also my responsibilities. Electric refrigerators were not to be found during the war so we had to settle for an icebox. The iceman carried a huge block with a tong on his leather-padded shoulder. Milkmen left the glass quarts outside the back door.

Mount Pleasant was like a small town. The shopping area at East 140th and Kinsman had a big A&P market, a butcher shop, and the original home of the popular Italian bakery Alesci's. Mother and I would take jars of collected fried fat saved for the military to the butcher where I shuffled on the sawdust-covered floor. As twilight began, I would return home with freshly baked Italian bread. Our Italian neighbor would give me Roma tomatoes from his bountiful garden.

My father did not learn to drive until 1951; instead, we rode the trolley. At nine I was allowed to go downtown alone to scout for new clothes. I strolled to every department store, registering in my head the clothes I would take my father to see and buy a week later. While downtown, we often saw movies at the awe-inspiring Hippodrome.

But Mount Pleasant had memorable amenities: spumoni ices, a Jewish deli, several synagogues, St. Cecilia's Church steps where we hung out, the Council Educational Alliance, a Jewish community center where my brother Burt, a soda jerk nicknamed "Brooklyn" for his accent, charmed the teenage women at the canteen. I, on the other hand, received five years of speech therapy at Fulton to transfer my accent to our Cleveland pronunciation.

The Mount Pleasant Public Library became my retreat. I read all the books in the youth section and most of the adolescent selections. After my baby sister Barbara was born, I checked out picture books for her. During the war I tended a Victory Garden and grew some vegetables in the driveway's narrow dirt edge. (See the photographs preserved on the Cleveland Memory Project at the CSU website.)

Sunday afternoons we took the trolley to the museums and cultural gardens. At nine, I was allowed to join the Conservation Club at the Museum of Natural History, riding the trolley after school and coming home after dark. One year my friend Barbara and I had scholarships to the Cleveland Institute of Art. She and I painted a mural that remained in the front hallway for years.

On summer afternoons the children on our block would form teams and play baseball until dark. Parents would toss coins wrapped in paper to the sidewalks for ice cream from the Good Humor Man. I rode my bike all over the neighborhood—to the Colony Theater on Shaker Square, to the nearby schoolyards in Shaker Heights, to the fancy Lee-Harvard area where I envied those people who lived in single homes.

My mother was popular. She organized Mahjong games. She hosted parties. The shopkeepers always greeted my mom and dad, grateful for the gift of her amazing baked pastries.

The war ended and the neighborhood was grateful as the soldiers came home. My mother wondered why no one was dancing in the street, as they would be doing in Brooklyn.

The real estate investors took advantage of the liberalized climate after the war that affected public institutions, hotels, and hospitals. More people of color moved to Mount Pleasant from the Central and other areas to find nicer apartments or houses, and real estate agents used "block busting" technique, to turn neighborhoods quickly. Whites panicked. They moved to the eastern suburbs because of fear of what were called the "undesirable Negroes" who would be taking over the neighborhood. My father took on extra work to purchase a home in University Heights. Prejudice led Shaker Heights city officials to change the name of Kinsman Road to Chagrin Blvd. at the Cleveland boundary, not wanting to be associated with the black neighborhoods. Shaker Heights erected concrete barriers that still exist where Cleveland streets enter Shaker.

My first day in eighth grade at Monticello Junior High in the Heights was disappointing. As a young teen, I questioned why there were no people of color in the Heights schools. I remember telling my parents "this is an inadequate educational setting for me." Even then I knew that segregation leads to social injustice, racism, and impoverishment.

Once the neighborhood became all black, landlords subdivided houses into small apartments and raised the rent exorbitantly. Mount Pleasant became a crowded ghetto of deteriorating housing and segregated schools.

I fail to understand why officials who could direct aid that would improve living conditions and restore the historical richness of the 1940s ignore the Mount Pleasant neighborhood. I often drive by and see the vacant dirty lots and boarded houses on East 139th. I read about tragic shootings and the terrible presence of the illegal drug trade. I spoke to an elderly woman whose parents bought a home on East 139th in the early 1950s. When asked if she feared living there alone, she said that some residents watch out for her and attempt to isolate her from the blight around her.

The remodeled Mt. Pleasant Public Library serves as a stable landmark. The stately Robert Fulton School is boarded. Hamilton Junior was torn down. Children no longer have the stability of neighborhood schools, healthy home environments, and the presence of small businesses and gardens to enjoy.

Today, trying to prevent further neighborhood deterioration, The Mount Pleasant Community Council and block clubs fight delinquency, crime, and housing violations. Cleveland Now and the Murtis Taylor Human Services System provide recreation and social services for the residents, but the urban crisis continues.

At the beginning of the 20th century, there was no black ghetto in Cleveland. By the middle of the 20th century, Mount Pleasant and probably most Cleveland neighborhoods had people living in slum conditions. Cleveland has yet to address the alienation and fear poisoning large areas of the city. It is a challenge to be embraced and not avoided. ◀

Best Boutiques & Thrifting

BY CLAIRE McMILLAN
Author of *The Gilded Age*

Juicy Lucy carries Parisian designer Isabel Marant (her clothes are coveted and hard to find), Cacharal, Yohiji Yamamamoto, and a discerning selection of avant-garde Belgian designers. Where the east side chicly low key yoga moms who aren't into labels shop. They carry Cleveland-based jewelry maker Todd Pownell's jewelry line of stackable rings and bracelets that look like you might have unearthed them from your backyard, if your backyard had diamonds in it.

Evie Lou Former *Plain Dealer* style columinst Kim Crow's store in Tremont has a large selection edited with an eye toward comfort, creativity, and the way we live in Cleveland. Carries cult brands Rundholz black label and Pas de Calais (also stocked at Barneys). She thoughtfully buys in a lot of larger sizes and at an array of price points. Almost anyone can find a thrill here. She and her staff are super friendly and not at all pushy.

Anne van H Arty, unique clothes, Anne is in the shop most days and is a pro at handing you the items in the shop that will fit your body type beautifully. The fun jewelry selection is particularly interesting and unique.

Deering Vintage/Gallery Jeffrey Cynthia Deering is a Cleveland legend in vintage and knows her stuff. She's had many locations and her fans always find her. She's got a great eye for nostalgia and the quirky. Treasures from the closets of Cleveland clothes-horses past can be found here.

Cleveland Consignment It's luxury labels only please at Suzie Vitale's well-edited shop, located at the cross roads of Hunting Valley, Chagrin Falls, and Pepper Pike. All the big names are well accounted for here with Chanel handbags, Prada shoes, Gucci sunglasses, and a large array of cocktail and evening dresses. She has a fur event every winter with a diverse and impressively large selection.

Unique Thrift Many locations thorough out NEO but those in the know agree that the location at 3333 Lorain is the best place to find buried treasures.

Lingg Heidi Lingg's shop has a distinctly directional point of view and it's reflected in the cool-girl jewelry and assorted clever gifts in the shop. A great place to pick up something to bring the hostess or to gift your sister for her birthday. I once spotted Michael Symon choosing gifts for his entire staff.

Both **Todd Pownell** and **Heather Moore**, who sell their jewelry nationally have studios in downtown Cleveland. They aren't open to the public but as mentioned, Pownell can be found at Juicy Lucy and Heather Moore's necklaces are sold at Hedges in Chagrin Falls.

Pretty Gritty:
Living Off Lorain Avenue

LEE CHILCOTE

My wife Katherine and I got married in 2006, and we bought a house at West 58th and Lorain, in the EcoVillage neighborhood, soon after that. We liked the area because it seemed urban and safe without being too trendy, and we could walk to theaters, bars, and coffee shops in the Gordon Square Arts District. We thought if we moved to Ohio City we'd have been surrounded by 25-year-old techies making $100K a year, or empty nesters from Solon who'd decided it would be fun to walk to the wine bar now that the kids were out of the house. We wanted to live in a more "authentic" urban neighborhood.

We purchased a townhouse in a row of new, "green" homes built close to the street. The local Community Development Corporation (CDC) was then touting EcoVillage as a model green neighborhood close to the Rapid station. They held a ribbon-cutting ceremony to celebrate its completion. There were stilt walkers, Great Lakes beer, and speeches by politicians about "revitalizing the neighborhood." Our unit was 2,400 square feet with a garden-level apartment, a large kitchen, a walk-in closet, and two and a half baths. The heating bills were under $50 a month and there was no backyard to mow.

By the time our moving truck showed up, though, private and public investors had already shifted their attention north to Gordon Square, where they were putting in new sidewalks, streetlights, and artistically shaped benches. Turns out we had made a bad call. Much of the promised investment in our area came slowly or never materialized at all. The vacant lot across the street stayed a vacant lot. Slumlords rented to the same crazies every year. The house across the street lost its gutters, the smell of weed wafted from the ratty couch on our neighbor's porch, and the guys who nodded at us outside the corner store weren't just being friendly. We had chosen to live in a part of the city that was falling apart and might never recover.

The $200,000, well-insulated, two-by-six construction EcoVillage townhomes became targets of crime. On the northwest corner of Lorain and 58th, there is a squat, cinderblock building that contains the Lorain Supermarket. The name is a bit of a misnomer since it mostly sells beer, junk food, and expired milk, quarts of which lurk in the bottom of coolers, but it is the only grocery store in the immediate neighborhood. Most who lived within walking distance used that store, including criminals, and took the dimly lit alley behind our homes to get there. Thieves robbed our neighbors at gunpoint, scampered over our fences to try to steal our air conditioning units, and even sliced open one of our garage doors with a saw like a tin can.

Our first summer there, my bike was stolen when I left my garage door open for five minutes while cleaning my patio. The cop who took the report berated me for living in the neighborhood, telling me point blank that I should move to the suburbs.

"Do you have any suggestions for making our units more secure?" I asked.

"Put snipers on the balconies," he said, shaking his head.

Right across from the Lorain Supermarket stood three deteriorating buildings that should have been condemned. The one on the corner was especially striking—a brick Victorian with carved stonework. There were still tenants living in it, including a family of five, and the building was being used for a drug dealing and prostitution ring. When the city finally condemned it, the landlord, who had moved to Atlanta as I recall, sold it for $10,000 to a couple who planned to renovate it for some kind of green architecture/interior design business. The couple was earnest and nice, but the house was soaked through with water from holes in the roof. They wrapped the house in a giant blue tarp while they tried to figure out a plan. Once, flying into Cleveland from visiting my in-laws in Kansas City, I looked out from the plane and saw it shimmering below like some kind of abstract public art piece. Shit, I thought, you can see the eyesore in my neighborhood from space.

A few months later, a piece of the building fell onto the sidewalk. Fortunately, no one was hurt, but the city had to tear it down. Yet doing so removed the only thing between us and Lorain Avenue, and left us exposed to people tagging our building and urinating on our vinyl siding.

When our roof started leaking, we started making exit plans. I soon learned that the construction company, D-A-S Construction, was out of business, the CEO in jail for bribing county officials. Cuyahoga County was in the middle of a corruption scandal, as two politicians were caught taking kickbacks in exchange for contracts. Although EcoVillage wasn't involved in the scandal, our contractor had screwed up the building's exterior, and an independent assessment showed that tens of thousands of dollars in repairs were needed.

So even as EcoVillage continued to be touted as a "nationally recognized green neighborhood," water soaked our new insulation and drywall. The CDC and architect eventually contributed toward fixing the roof, but it only covered a small percentage of the cost, and we had to sign an agreement saying that we wouldn't sue the CDC.

Despite its challenges, the main strip, Lorain Avenue between West 25th and West 65th, retains a certain romance, ungentrified and with great architecture. Some shops, like the Hot Dog Inn, a slender storefront where you can get a chili dog for $1.50, and Steve's Lunch, where you could walk in and find punk rockers drinking coffee next to prostitutes at one in the morning, seemed like they'd been there since the dawn of time. (Steve's Lunch burned down in 2015.) The merchants are hard-bitten urban pioneers. Nook n Cranny is an antique store jammed with old lamps and shades at the corner of West 52nd and Lorain. The first time I went in there, the furnace was out and the owner had an industrial blower perched on a shelf. It was 15 degrees outside, but he had no plans to fix it.

I understand now that the city is divided into winning and losing neighborhoods. If one lives in an area close to downtown or a major employment center, with some historic wealth and good housing stock, an on-the-ball councilperson who returns phone calls, and a functional CDC, then you're good. Otherwise, even if you read the brochures, look at the sales comps, and meet your potential neighbors, if there is a recession and the economy shrugs and dies, your little working-class enclave held together by love and aluminum siding, where white, black, and Puerto Rican families pass barbeque over their fences, might lose.

Eventually, we moved five blocks away to the Gordon Square Arts District, buying an old Victorian on a street with young families. The romance of urban pioneering may have gotten the best of us the first time, but we are committed to learning from experience. Or maybe we're just stubborn, and that cop telling me to leave made me that much more determined to stay. ◄

Best Places to Live

Housing is arguably the best reason to live in Cleveland, although it is so on the backs of misfortune: prices are low and options are plentiful.

Lakewood This west side inner-ring suburb's houses, bars, and restaurants flank the lake, as does its beautiful and popular Lakewood Park.

Cleveland Heights An inner-ring suburb on the east side popular with Case Western Reserve University students and staff, Cleveland Heights is stocked with century-old brick housing.

Ohio City Arguably the trendiest neighborhood in town, Ohio City offers the West Side Market, dozens of bars, and short bike rides over the Hope Memorial Bridge to downtown.

Tremont This former steel workers' village now attracts an eclectic mix of younger and older residents, with plenty of shops and restaurants within walking distance.

Detroit Shoreway The west side's newest hip neighborhood, Detroit Shoreway is popular with artists, activists, and folks headed to a lecture and beers at the Happy Dog.

Larchmere/Shaker Square Within the city limits (and thus lower Cleveland taxes), this neighborhood mixes antique shops, condos, houses and restaurants, all right by the Rapid.

Slavic Village Centrally located and redolent with history, Slavic Village actively assists and welcomes new home buyers.

Asiatown/Campus District Lined with beautiful brick factories, the streets of this midtown neighborhood are striking and affordable.

North Collinwood One of the few places in Cleveland where you can live on the water.

Sweet Spot in the City

DIANE MILLETT

When I was nine years old, I developed an allergy to lake water — or sweetwater as my parents sometimes called it. It marked the end of summers at our family's cottage on a lake in New Hampshire. Even though I was just a kid, I had become attached to the smell and feel of being on the water in ways I did not realize until I was much older. Little did I know that some 45 years later I would be lucky enough to once again have a lake in my front yard.

In 2004, by accident or sweet serendipity, my life partner stumbled upon a house for sale in North Collinwood on Lake Erie in a neighborhood we barely knew existed. Knowing I often dreamed of living on the water, she arranged for us to look at it. We drove from our large home in Cleveland Heights to a North Collinwood neighborhood and gazed at the water, hardly seeing the house. I felt like the lake was opening its heart, showing us its blue-gray waves stretching all the way to Canada and wrapping us in a fluid embrace. We were in. By midnight we had a signed purchase agreement.

It was a hasty decision. We had lived in Cleveland Heights for over two decades. We weren't in the market for a new house and hadn't yet decided what we would do at retirement, which was not too many years off. We aren't originally from Cleveland, but over the years we had come to love the area and our Cleveland friends. Still, did we want to stay here after retirement?

The house in North Collinwood was a small, mid-century brick ranch with sturdy bones but in need of serious renovation. It had its strengths: it was one story (no stairs for our aging bodies), and it had a two-car attached garage (important in our view for living in Cleveland). The realty listing included the house and the vacant land across the street; a grassy stretch about 65 feet deep with a 15-foot plus drop to the water.

We knew our view of the lake would remain unobstructed because we would own the waterfront land. It had us with that.

We learned about the neighborhood over the months before we moved and in the years since. North Collinwood is an easy 20-minute drive from downtown and University Circle. It is perfect for commutes to work, the orchestra, the art museum, the theater district, sporting venues and first-class medical care. In 2004, the Waterloo area in North Collinwood was emerging as a haven for artists and music lovers with Beachland Ballroom at its core. Nowadays, Waterloo is well known as a major Arts and Entertainment District. The foodie scene was developing back then with the new Bistro 185 alongside older stalwarts like Muldoon's and Scotti's. Now we have The Standard, Cleveland Brewery and a major plan for the redevelopment of East 185th Street including the vintage LaSalle Theater.

North Collinwood is a big residential area and our house is in a little neighborhood in the northeast corner. We border Wildwood Metropark on one side, East 185th Street on another; the neighborhood fronts on Lake Erie.

As we got to know neighbors and became known to them, we learned that our fears about not being accepted here as a gay couple were unfounded. This is an old, ethnic neighborhood that now holds the hearts of urban pioneers and oldsters who resisted flight to the suburbs. We found tolerance, acceptance and a caring community. The shared love of the water holds us together.

We learned that the East Shore Park Club, a private club founded in the early 1900s, would be our anchor. Beach clubs are a unique feature of communities along Lake Erie. In our 10 years here we've attended or volunteered to help with Oktoberfests, clambakes, pancake breakfasts, steak dinners, soup nights, and Fourth of July picnics. During warm weather, we have a Thursday night summer concert series bringing neighbors together to enjoy music, picnics and wine while watching the sunset. When we invite friends from the Heights or other suburbs to join us for these events or parties, many say things like, "This is Cleveland?" "I never knew this was here!" "What neighborhood is this again?"

It didn't take long to realize that lakefront dwellers generally stop what they are doing to watch the lake, whatever it is doing. We watch the fishing boats, freighters, sailing regattas and cigarette boats; we grab our binoculars for eagles, ducks, herons, and gulls. We stop to watch as monarchs and warblers land on our zinnias, exhausted from their flight across the lake on their trek south. We watch storms moving across the lake, coming down from Canada; we watch and take photos of clouds and sun reflecting off the lake; we watch waves breaking over rocks and crashing on the shore; we watch the water become viscous as it freezes and thaws.

And always, we watch the sunsets. From our house, we can see the sunset every day of the year. We watch the sky, the horizon, and the colors — shades of pastels reflecting off the surface of the lake — while the sun sinks into the water.

Sometimes I have to pinch myself to believe it is real: the lake in our front yard — this vast body of water that shows us its moods and wraps us in the sounds and sights of its ever-changing surface. After all these years, I've rediscovered sweetwater and discovered a sweet spot in Cleveland. ◀

homage to...

On the Rise Artisan Breads

The artisanal breads and pastries at On the Rise bakery are among the best this side of the Atlantic. The olive loaves are as soft as they are flavorful, the cinnamon raisin bread has a yeasty sweetness, and the baguettes have just the right crunch. The scones are sprinkled with some secret ingredient that compels you to return the next day, perhaps to have an apricot croissant, a sticky bun, or brownie. And if you spend too much of the morning hanging out at the large wooden communal table chatting with the regulars, you can stay for lunch—but that would involve choosing between the equally excellent roast beef or prosciutto sandwiches.

On Fairmount Boulevard in Cleveland Heights, On The Rise is flanked by several other lovely locally owned businesses, and the block has an oddly quaint feel—it's been called "an outpost of Greenwich, Connecticut" and "the westernmost block of the East Coast." Once you hit Lee Road, apparently, you are in the Midwest.

Wherever it reminds you of, and whatever you order, be sure to try their coffee; the mysterious excellence of On The Rise extends to their brew, too.

When Your Neighborhood Just Can't Get No Respect

SALLY MARTIN

have a confession to make. I live in South Euclid and think it's pretty freaking awesome. This shouldn't seem like a shocking revelation except that South Euclid has a pesky self-esteem problem, and a lot of people who might agree with that statement are embarrassed to admit it. In the eight years since becoming the city's Housing Manager, I've become convinced that what the city needs most is a motivational speaker. Recently, at a community development conference, we were asked an intriguing question: if your city or neighborhood was a famous person, who would it be? It didn't take me long to realize that in spite of our community's many wonderful amenities, Rodney Dangerfield was the obvious answer. South Euclid gets no respect from the region and even, at times, from its own residents. The bigger question is how did the collective self-esteem of a community get so low in the first place?

As a resident myself since 2001, I struggle to understand. It seems that if you're not originally from here, your opinion is vastly different and far more positive than that of most of the "lifers." From my standpoint, after living in five states, South Euclid is a pretty amazing place to call home.

The history of South Euclid mirrors the history of many of Northeast Ohio's inner-ring suburbs. As newer communities were built further out, some folks left in search of greener pastures. This decades-long out-migration trend has left inner-ring suburbs with a nasty "sprawl hangover." A smaller population means comparatively high tax rates and fewer resources to maintain the existing infrastructure. But being the resourceful people that we are, we've found many innovative ways to fight back and retain our vibrancy. In spite of the challenges, there are some very compelling reasons to call this place home.

South Euclid is close to everything. We can get to University Circle, downtown, the hospitals, shopping, and wonderful restaurants in minutes. We have our own slice of the emerald necklace, as a large section of the Cleveland Metroparks Euclid Creek Reservation runs through the city. The new Acacia Reservation is just five minutes away in Lyndhurst. And South Euclid has one of the region's oldest venues for live jazz — The House of Swing on Mayfield Road.

South Euclid is affordable and inherently "green." We have well-built homes with great architectural diversity and many of them will set you back less than $100,000. Like all inner-ring suburbs, foreclosures took a toll on housing values. Since the housing crisis began in 2006, 20 percent of South Euclid's housing stock has been in foreclosure.

Compounding that, the decades-long trend of population loss has resulted in the low sale prices we see in our market today. Even though sale prices are affordable, rents are disproportionately high. Average rents on a single-family home run between $1,000 and $1,250 per month. The city has effectively managed the housing crisis, taking an aggressive stance against blight by passing an innovative vacant building ordinance, using strategic demolition, and by establishing a community development corporation, One South Euclid. The city ranks highly on many area "best value" lists, and was named a Keller-Williams Top 10 Community in 2014. Most of our homes are under 2,000 square feet (although there are some mansions too) and they're affordable to live in. Thanks to demolition and some federal grant funds, there are now eight community gardens throughout the city and sidewalks are everywhere, making South Euclid a highly walkable community. New construction is taking place throughout the city as well. Brand new homes range from $180,000 to $250,000 — much less than comparable construction in outlying communities.

South Euclid is transit friendly. It's easy to catch a bus and get anywhere, and rail is nearby too. This fact has allowed my developmentally disabled sister to gain a huge measure of independence, and it's a great amenity for anyone wanting to cut back on driving and live a more sustainable lifestyle.

South Euclid is diverse. For many of us, raising our families in a place where not everyone looks alike is a major selling point, and as of the last census, our community of 23,000 stands at a 60/40 ratio of white to black. Over the past few years, a growing population of Bhutanese refugees also now call South Euclid home. A new Bhutanese grocery store has opened on Mayfield Road and the city has a community garden, the Victory Friendship Garden, devoted to meeting their dietary needs with affordable, fresh produce.

South Euclid-Lyndhurst Schools are great. This is a hotly contested point and an area where that self-esteem problem comes in. As more lower-income folks began moving in and using the schools, we saw a shift in the demographics of our school district, as many middle-class residents decided to send their children to private schools. Our schools no longer match the demographics of either community they serve. Both South Euclid and Lyndhurst remain predominately white and middle class, although the level of diversity in both cities continues to increase. As a result of the increased poverty levels of the schools, test scores and state rankings have decreased. It was a self-fulfilling prophecy—as residents convinced each other that the schools were no good and decided to flee, it became clear, based on the ratings, that they had indeed become far worse, except that the numbers don't tell the whole story.

Not much has fundamentally changed about the curriculum at the district since it had excellent ratings just a decade ago. District-wide, there are more than 30 AP and honors classes, scores of extracurricular offerings, a STEM program, opportunities to earn free college credit while in high school, 58 sports teams, a gorgeous stadium, and world-class music and art instruction. There's even a farm-to-fork program that brings local produce to our cafeterias, and the impressive Excel Tech program, that allows students real-world training in over 22 vocations. It's not a stretch to say that if all of our residents decided to start sending their kids to the district, our rankings would quickly be back to where they were 12 years ago. As a school parent myself, I can attest to the remarkable outcomes I see with my own children and many others that I have the privilege of writing about on the SEL Experience Project blog.

South Euclid is home to remarkable people. Although it would come as a surprise to many people, on my street alone, there's a record producer (Ringo Starr has been a frequent house guest!), a Cleveland Orchestra musician, two award-winning writers, a landscape photographer, the founder of a nationally recognized branding firm, a toy inventor, and myriad other cool folks. The problem is, many of them think they are alone. Ask them where they live and they might sheepishly tell you, "on the east side." ◀

Observatory, Sea Monster

DOUGLAS MAX UTTER

As if the sky had fallen, down the street
from my house, at the top of a ridge
The wreck of an observatory
rolls toward northern constellations;

(a groundhog scratches through the Pleiades,
a coyote keeps to the
shadows near Cassiopeia)

Down the hill feverish cash-green salons
Fluoresce, an ailanthus wraps the steps,
Runs its roots along splintered sills.
At dusk young deer shrink through new wilderness.

From the horizon comes
Flashing at the lake shore;
Our own sea in chains thrashing,
a Cetus or Leviathan -- defiant with a mighty tail,
slipping off the hook;

twists and slaps, pied against the break wall.

The Opposite of Cool

GEORGE MOUNT

There's an effort in Cleveland to recreate what it once was: a city of integrated neighborhoods valuing culture, family, and civic pride. But I often feel no sense of continuity with the past in these urban enclaves. Few of the hippest restaurants and coffee shops have been around for more than a few years. Emblematic of this difficulty to integrate the past are posh condominiums repurposed from closed schools and factories.

It's great to breathe new life into these structures, but unfortunate that many longtime residents, likely alumni of West Tech or long-ago Eveready employees, can't afford these luxury dwellings. This fracturing could make you wonder: can the neighborhoods of Cleveland grow stronger while respecting the past?

I believe the answer is "yes," and the proof is right over the 480 bridge at State Road. It's a place many urban pioneers reactively call the opposite of cool.

I live in Ukrainian Village, Parma. This stretch of State Road between Tuxedo and Grantwood was given this title in 2009, although this codified the obvious. Home to Ohio's largest Ukrainian population, it's got the Slavic flavor that makes this region unique.

Parma in the 1950s was the fastest-growing suburb in America. Postwar industrial workers resettled in the suburbs, and Parma, sitting on the city's southern border, close to a large manufacturing base, was the first stop. The Ukrainian community, previously based in Tremont, found a new hub in Parma, namely along State Road.

Of course, this suburban exodus contributed to Cleveland's population drain. Parma grew in the time of white flight, and remains mostly white. Fifty years after Parma's population boom, and sustained by continued immigration from the old country, Ukrainian Village retains its ethnic identity, with some smattering of black, Hispanic, and even Filipino influence.

Parma gets an unfair reputation: boring, gruff, slovenly. It's a big suburb — the biggest in Ohio — so sprawl does exist, especially the further from the Cleveland border you go. But Ukrainian Village, on the town's northern border, is a classic inner-ring suburban neighborhood. Unlike many others, it is livable in its own right, proving that there is a way to combine old-world customs, livable neighborhoods, and affordable housing.

Let's take a tour. Coming from the north, you will see the Basista Furniture sign towering over the neighborhood, one of several vintage neon signs dotting the block. These signs convey an attitude expressed by much of the village: "Hip or not, this damn sign works and we're using it." It's cool without trying to be cool.

Keep travelling up State and you'll see the glimmering domes of St. Josaphat and St. Vladimir, both Ukrainian churches. I joke that onion domes make the Parma skyline. Byzantine icons cover St. Vladimir Ukrainian Orthodox Cathedral, while mosaics dot St. Josaphat Ukrainian Catholic Cathedral.

These churches worship in the same rites as the old country. Very little has changed in Ukrainian liturgical worship, another instance of the "if it ain't broke, don't fix it" attitude that pervades the neighborhood. The services can last for two hours or longer, the majority of the time spent standing. At least there is plenty to occupy one's attention—the "smells and bells" of incense, icons, and chanting are meant to engage the whole person in prayer.

Like many ethnic churches, food is a staple for revenue and ministry. There are Ukrainian food festivals, weekly pierogi sales, and my favorite, Lenten fish fries. St. Josaphat hosts one in its former house of worship, known as the "Astrodome" for its arena-like architecture. Lines flow out the door, and it's worth the wait. St. Vladimir's also hosts a fish fry in its banquet hall, serving the usual fried fish and chowder but also Ukrainian items like pierogi and potato pancakes. I look forward every Lent to meeting family, friends, and neighbors at Parma's fish fries. There's no better way to start a cold, damp March weekend in Cleveland.

It is possible to buy your food like you would in the old country, in specialty stores, not at a supermarket. There are several bakeries, butcher shops, imported dry-goods stores and so forth. Nearly every storefront in Ukrainian Village is locally owned and operated, many of them ethnically Ukrainian.

People come from around Northeast Ohio for the old-fashioned kielbasa at State Meats. Demand peaks at Christmas and Easter, when the scent of smoked meats lingers in the air for blocks. The pierogi next door at Mama Maria's, a prepared-food deli run by State Meats, are fantastic. And a few storefronts down you can have more pierogis at Perla Homemade Delight. OK, kielbasa and pierogi aren't light; Slavic food is starchy and hearty, like the people.

Looking to buy? A well-maintained, 1,500-square-foot bungalow can go for under six figures, and the crime rate is well below that of most cities of the same population. And a quick bike ride or Uber gets you to Tremont or the Flats.

These days, I find myself giving my friends lots of tours. Beforehand, I get some groans: "It's so far! There's nothing to do!" But by the end the objections have usually been overturned. So for those looking to improve the city of Cleveland's neighborhoods, I salute you. But if you have never been to "boring" Parma, take a drive down State Road. It's not far, and there's a lot to admire. ◀

Best Breakfast

We all know that it's the most important meal of the day, so the last thing you want to do is to choose your source poorly.

Big Al's Diner People swear by the corned beef hash, but the rest of the menu will fill you up right too.

Lucky's Café Good all-day eatin', but breakfast is where it's at. Well-thought-out menu choices with a noticeably fresh feel (herbs and other ingredients come straight from the garden out back).

Nick's Diner The classic "greasy spoon." Typical diner food, done right. And cheap. They still rock a $2.99 breakfast special which is all the more tasty eaten under the funky art on the walls.

Jack Flaps A menu divided into "Sweet" and "Savory" helps you home in on what you crave. No matter how you choose you'll be in a happy place. Note: no groups larger than six on weekends.

Yours Truly Sure it's sort of a chain, but they are locally owned and an easy go-to when you know what you want, and what you want is consistency in taste, portion size, and service.

Gus's Family Restaurant You can't go wrong with a place that's been filling bellies for more than 30 years. Classic diner food, served with extra love.

Le Petit Triangle Café This ain't no greasy spoon. Trick your taste buds into thinking they woke up on Europe with a crepe, eclectically filled omelet, parfait, or croissant breakfast sandwich.

Inn on Coventry Fresh, homemade eating with friendly staff who make you feel like you are at home. Breakfast standards along with some more funky options.

Holton Avenue:
Kinsman's Other Corridor for Opportunities

GREGGOR MATTSON

Holton Avenue is one of only seven East-West streets that bridge the industrial zone dividing Cleveland's southeast neighborhoods, and only one of three that knits the two halves of Kinsman. Even after the vaunted Opportunity Corridor finally links I-490 to E. 105th, and despite its potholes, Holton will still be the fastest route to my boyfriend's apartment off Shaker Square.

Holton, precisely a mile long, is a microcosm of what Cleveland city planners call the "forgotten triangle." Over half the lots are vacant. Its seven churches are energetically named Deliverance, Evangelistic, New Hope, missionary and festival. The faded, flashy murals of the Intercity Truck and Car Wash overshadow the only other three businesses, all trucking-related. Single-family homes are as likely to be well-kempt as shabby; a couple are derelict. There's a small, bare park for hoops on the east side; its swingsets have no swings.

The city's industrial infrastructure is laid bare. Fire hydrants sprout in front of vacant lots. Utility poles march evenly past crumbling curbs. The distant erector set of a Cleveland Public Power substation rises from a vast field. Graffiti tags by 2TRAINZ bracket where the road dives under a freight rail line, itself spanned by twin rail bridges. Holton jogs through and under these mismatched siblings, the raw steel and concrete supports for the RTA lines to Shaker Heights a stark contrast with the alabaster Art Deco arches of the old Cleveland & Youngstown railroad, poetically described on an old postcard as a "concrete bridge performance." Some of the giant beams are stained with rust, others have orderly rivets offset by thick paint, but all of the raw brick and concrete underpasses are crumbling.

Less visible to passersby is Holton's social infrastructure. The many vacant lots are mowed and periodically cleaned of mattresses, tires and trash by the City and its land bank, which own about half the land. Only occasionally does barbecue smoke waft from the clubhouse for the mother chapter of the 'O'Mens motorcycle club, where swarms of shiny parked pickup trucks announce late night parties. A nearby warehouse was once the Horvath Brass Foundry and, until recently, still casting machine parts as the Electro Finishing Corporation. A low, overgrown brick wall marks the ruin of the parish school of St. Ladislaus, the first church for the city's

Slovaks. After it burned in 1970, the parish moved to Westlake. Another church building, once Hungarian Baptist, is now African American, its parking lot full on Sunday mornings.

At twilight, the encroaching forest is peaceful and full of crickets. I've seen deer, skunks, raccoons and a coyote. The dark of night and early morning witness darker passersby: a suspicious fire in an abandoned house, dogs dumped from moving cars, the naked body of a young man under a rail bridge, a fleeing woman just raped at gunpoint, and two gunfights outside the 'O'Mens clubhouse.

It would be easy to focus on these spectacular crimes, and a mistake to ignore them. Though this neighborhood is described by city planners as "one of the most connected in the city," there aren't that many of us passing through. The city planning office has slated a transit-oriented housing village for the Avenue's west end, and greenspace for the east. But because I've never gotten out of my car, I don't know what the souls of Holton Avenue think about how these proposals would affect them as they work, party, worship, listen and live. Though for whom is yet unclear, this corridor also has opportunities. ◀

SHILOH BAPTIST CHURCH

Excitement Sprouts in Hough

MANSFIELD FRAZIER

A long a quarter-mile corridor on E. 66th Street (running just north of Chester Avenue, continuing on to Lexington Avenue) three projects are redefining and bringing excitement to an historic part of the east side community of Hough, which is situated an equal distance between downtown and University Circle.

In 2010, a federally funded program entitled "Reimagining Cleveland" was launched with the stated goal of transforming our town into a "Green City on a Blue Lake." A weed choked, three-quarter acre vacant lot that had sat empty on the northwest corner of E. 66th and Hough for decades was transformed into The Vineyards of Château Hough, which now boasts 294 grapevines, planted in 14 rows; seven rows Traminette, a white grape from upstate New York, and seven rows of Frontenac, a red grape from Wisconsin—both of which are cold-hardy varieties that are able to withstand Cleveland's often harsh winters.

Then, a short two blocks away, League Park, which is heralded as the oldest baseball field in the world (it was built in 1891 as the home of Cleveland's first professional baseball team, the Spiders, and also was the park where Babe Ruth hit his famous 500th home run on August 12, 1929) was completely renovated in 2013 and now plays host to a wide variety of year-round events, in addition to regular summer baseball games.

Lastly, the October, 2014 Grand Opening of a unique structure called a "BioCellar"—the world's first underground greenhouse, a facility that's used as an experimental crop propagation and teaching space—completed the transformation of the corridor into what is fast becoming a "destination" attraction.

Local oenophiles, and a number of wine enthusiasts from around the world, now visit Château Hough—courtesy of a relationship established with the Cleveland Council on World Affairs in 2012—to sample the vineyard's Traminette-Viognier blend, which won a second place ribbon at the Great Geauga County Fair in 2013 with its very first vintage. Not long afterward, the vineyard was "liked" in O, The Oprah Magazine coverage that assisted greatly in raising the profile—in addition to establishing the reputation—of the project.

The BioCellar, which sits adjacent to the vineyard, is visited by students from primary grades through graduate school, from all points in the county, and has developed strong ties with Case Western Reserve University, where students from the Weatherhead School of Management examine the business model as a case study on socially responsible entrepreneurial enterprises. Additionally, a work/study program in conjunction with nearby Margaret Ireland High School (which is part of Cleveland school's Positive Education Program for students with behavioral problems) was embarked upon in 2015.

The overarching goal is to create an "urban agriculture zone"—complete with a winery that's on the drawing board—that achieves a triple-net bottom line of: repurposing vacant land and buildings; growing environmentally friendly products; and creating jobs for neighborhood residents, thereby assisting in strengthening the social fabric of the Hough community.

Now, when tourists on Lolly the Trolley ride past this urban oasis on their way to visit League Park, they smile, wave and wonder, "just what the heck is going on in this part of Hough?" ◀

Best Places to Buy Locally Grown Food

Cleveland is a fertile city for produce lovers, and the region is replete with small farmers who sell their wares around town.

Fresh Fork Market An inventive twist on Community Supported Agriculture, Fresh Fork Market curates the best from a wide swath of farmers and puts together a bag of veggies, meat, canned, and frozen goods for you to pick up year round.

Green Corps The Cleveland Botanical Gardens hires high school students to work in urban farms around the city and sells the produce they grow at farmers markets in Kinsman, Midtown and other spots, watering food deserts.

North Union Farmer's Market This Shaker Square Saturday market offers the same reliable weekly experience as church going does for others. Here you can find flowers, tomatoes, pickles, and friends who have stopped shopping to chat.

West Side Market This iconic Cleveland market houses some vendors whose produce was not grown nearby, but it is also the venue for local small businesses who will sell you their 216-produced sausage, pasta, Russian tea biscuits, and other local specialities.

Ohio City Farm One of the country's largest urban farms, Ohio City Farms is worked by refugees from Nepal, Bhutan, and Somalia as well as folks from the Cleveland Metropolitan Housing Authority and Cleveland Crops' adults with developmental disabilities. The farm stand can be hard to find, but it's worth the search.

Chasing the Ghosts of Coventry Village

BRAD MASI

I. GHOST STREAMS

Late May, the cusp of summer, I glide down the brushy side streets of Cleveland Heights. My bicycle jiggles over the occasional stretch of brick road, reminding me that pavement was originally invented to make biking easier.

I'm biking to Coventry Village, the Bohemian epicenter of Cleveland Heights, a swirling mixture of antiques, vintage toys, head shops, churches, grocers, hardware stores, funky imports, indie rock bands, revolutionary and countercultural books, cafes, acting schools, sports bars and culinary options that stretch from middle America to East Asia. They even have a place where you can get locked in a room and forced to solve complex riddles to escape.

A haven for the easily distracted, Coventry often lures me in with a simple mission in mind, perhaps a jaunt to Heights Hardware to fetch a screw for an ailing cabinet back home. An hour later, I find myself clutching a handful of Star Wars figures from Big Fun while wolfing down a bowl of French onion soup at Tommy's, hoping to make a poetry reading at Mac's Backs that I just found out about. At some point, it occurs to me that I never made it to the hardware store for that damn screw.

But today, I am in pursuit of a different kind of meandering adventure in Coventry—a hike along Dugway Brook, which runs right through the center of Coventry Village. On the surface, this sounds like a particularly challenging, if not delusional, quest, as there is no actual water visible.

Roy Lerick, a local anthropologist, leads the search for this "ghost stream," his description of a historic stream that has disappeared underground, locked away in concrete culverts beneath the hapless footfalls of the denizens above.

Roy leads our motley band of natural historians, bird watchers, history buffs, and extreme hikers like a docent through the Land of the Lost. The contemporary facade of Coventry fades as our group shuffles through the bustling stream of shoppers and casual strollers. With an urgent gait, Roy makes a beeline to the least spectacular landmark in Coventry, a three-story parking garage that gobbled up a lot of good urban space to make the district accessible to our heavily motorized public.

Roy arrives at a densely wooded area along a ridge behind the parking garage, pointing to a sandstone outcropping that rises amid a mix of dirt, ivy and urban detritus: plastic bags, discarded condoms, snack bags and other washed-up souvenirs of our disposable culture.

The stone formations rise like the scepters of the vast inland sea that covered the Cleveland Metropolitan area 350 million years ago. At that time, the land that would become Cleveland resided around the latitude of Peru, part of Pangaea, the contiguous land mass that preceded continental drift. I imagine the Appalachian Mountains towering on the horizon, slowly eroding into this sea. Wave action piled sand from these mountains into beaches and shallow shores. Compressed over geological time, these beaches became the sandstone formations in front of us, the lost guardians of Pangaea, relegated to their post behind Coventry Garage.

Coventry Village sits in a geologically dynamic space, a terrace that perches about 300 feet above the flat Lake Plains that define much of Cleveland. Underlying this terrace is a bedrock layer unique to Northeast Ohio: bluestone. It is encountered perhaps most frequently in the sidewalks that make Cleveland Heights so walkable. Roy runs Bluestone Heights, an educational organization whose name comes from this bedrock edifice upon which many of the inner-ring suburbs perch. Roy looks at the Heights not as a tangle of zip codes and municipalities but as an integrated complex of communities united by a shared geological legacy and a series of parallel streams that each form their own exclusive small watershed that drains into Lake Erie.

For Coventry, this stream is Dugway, whose patient erosion over the 14,000 years since the glaciers receded revealed these sandstone formations and shaped the land on which Coventry sits. Roy takes us from the parking garage, promising to give us a glimpse of this elusive stream.

We arrive at the intersection of Coventry and Lancashire Roads, where Roy stops at a sewer grating. A trio of Jehovah's Witnesses stand beside the grating with a table weighed down with flyers promising salvation. Roy describes the route of the stream right where we are standing, tracing remnants in the landscape around us. As he speaks, the undulations of the stream's ancestral banks become suddenly noticeable in the terrain of parking lots, sidewalks, and yards.

I find myself strangely saddened by the disappearance of this once-great waterway. Pedestrians shuffle by, dodging the Jehovah's Witnesses and our strange band of ghost stream chasers, oblivious to the ancient legacy that lies underfoot. I long for a glimpse of what once used to be here.

Just then, Jim Miller, a local stream specialist also on the tour, produces a four-foot length of PVC pipe and places it at the top of the sewer grating. We take turns cupping our ears to the top of the pipe, the sound of the rushing stream below suddenly amplified over the traffic, crowds, and urgent proselitizing.

The sound of the stream connects me to a more ancient spirit of Coventry. At that moment, I understand what Roy referred to as "deep history," a recognition that Cleveland is not a recent construct, but rather the culmination of an ancient natural legacy woven together with more recent urban settlement. Understanding this legacy connects us to a dynamic world bigger than ourselves that calls for our responsible stewardship.

A few hundred feet from where we stand, Dugway Brook opens up and tumbles down a gorge of grey-hewn bluestone in Lakeview Cemetery. It is a fleeting moment where the stream recovers its untrammeled natural glory before being channeled into a concrete flood control dam, a monument of Soviet-style brutalism that sits strangely in the center of the cemetery.

Down from the Dugway gorge, tombstones perch delicately upon the steep descent of the Portage Escarpment, the terminus of the bedrock formation that gives the Heights its stature before the descent into the Lake Plain of Cleveland. A scan of the tombstones here provides a jumbled account of Cleveland history, one that includes Civil War generals, U.S. Presidents, 22 Cleveland mayors, and one comic book anti-hero from Coventry who's raspy voice can almost be heard reading his epitaph: "Life is about women, gigs, and bein' creative." Like Dugway brook, comics writer Harvey Pekar has shaped the contours of the rich literary landscape around Coventry.

II. GHOST WRITERS

In the same way that Dugway was forced to the oblivion of its underground channel, Cleveland's literary scene has similarly faced a history of suppression. And like Dugway Brook, finding that moment for its true, natural expression in the bluestone gorge of Lakeview Cemetery, Coventry serves as a node for the free flow of ideas and expression in Cleveland.

Many writers, poets, artists, publishers, and graphic novelists find their home here and many more were hatched here before their winged migration to other territories. The legacy of two pioneers of literary expression and free speech can be found here and, like good ghosts, remain at the edges where you have to look a bit to find them. To see them, and understand the urban history of Cleveland that each embodied in their work, it is best to be on foot.

On a beautiful July morning, I tramped down the backstreets of Coventry, worried about missing the opening dedication of Pekar Park, a monument to Harvey Pekar's work. Aided by the steep decline of the Portage Escarpment, I hustled down the brick-covered Mornington Lane as it flowed into Euclid Heights Boulevard. As I often do, I skipped halfway across the street, then made my way along the grassy, tree-lined median to Coventry.

The median fills me with a strange nostalgia for a part of Cleveland that I never experienced. What seems an aesthetic flourish to dampen traffic, these medians once served as the corridors for an extensive electric streetcar network that connected neighborhoods throughout Cleveland. These medians occur throughout Cleveland Heights, a streetcar suburb, which hit its initial growth period in the 1920s, a time when private automobiles were mostly the province of wealthier classes. Then, people walked, biked or took streetcars. Cleveland Heights still retains the basic bones of a walkable and transit-oriented urban environment as a result.

As I approach Coventry Boulevard, I cross over the remaining half of the boulevard and stride toward a small gathering of people circulating among canopies and a makeshift stage on an open peninsula of land in front of the Grog Shop, a haven for indie bands. I pause to admire the marvel of the curved architecture looming above the crowd as apartments along the Boulevard seamlessly flow into Coventry's retail district. This arc of buildings serves as a ghost relic of the streetcar line as it curved north onto Coventry Road. As a fixed rail system, streetcars could not make sharp turns. Instead, they made wide arcs to gradually shift direction, a common urban design pattern encountered in Cleveland Heights.

With the streetcars gone, this bonus piece of open land has, since the 1960s, served as a neighborhood gathering and performance space, as Coventry shifted from a predominantly Jewish neighborhood to the center of Cleveland's counterculture scene. But, recently, this space had been busted up by the installation of concrete planters and barricades installed to discourage community assembly. The loss of this space particularly struck Harevy Pekar's wife Joyce Brabner, who recalled that the spot used to be a "haven for nonconformist and creative youth until overblown anxiety about flash mobs and kids hanging around without money to support local business led to curfews and what many felt was repressive redesign." Through the park, Joyce saw an opportunity to return the area to "its earlier, youth- and arts-friendly state by removing the big blocky 'people bumper' planters that were installed to discourage assembly, and welcome back young people, street musicians, storytellers, chess players and others to a communal meeting and gathering space."

But the space has a much deeper personal connection for Joyce and many others who recall the space as a nexus for the kind of communal artistic expression that propelled her husband's work. At the opening ceremony, Joyce described how "Harvey really loved moving into Coventry because that's the place where he felt like he was a writer, he was creative, and the kinds of things that he was about were appreciated."

Joyce describes how "Harvey used to walk down from his apartment on Hampshire to this corner where everyone would hang out and he would stand there and tell stories like a stand-up comedy routine." She also pointed out his likely ulterior motive of "impressing girls." Nestled among the trees, a series of banners line the park as an ambulatory comic strip, each capturing a scene of Harvey's life in Cleveland.

The dedication of the park brought in an assembly of people a variety of ages who recalled their interactions with Harvey. Steve Presser, owner of Big Fun, recalled watching Harvey constantly going in and out of his apartment, often clutching piles of albums, used books, or gesticulating wildly as he talked to himself. Joyce later pointed out that this was how Harvey would sometimes reenact dialogue for his stories.

As I listened to people's recollections, my attention drifted to the stately marquee for the Centrum Theater just beyond the park. Now a church, the theater previously went by the name of the "Heights Art Theater," a common location featured in many of Harvey's comics. In 1959, police raided the theater and arrested its manager for screening the French film *The Lovers*, which the county prosecutor deemed obscene. The case made its way to the Supreme Court, which upheld the rights for the film to be screened, putting Cleveland at the epicenter of national efforts to protect free expression from the country's more puritanical urges.

Ten years later, Cleveland poet d.a. levy was arrested for distributing poetry deemed obscene by the same county prosecutor. The prosecution of levy drew Allen Ginsberg, who himself survived court efforts to censor "Howl," to Cleveland to defend levy's right to free expression amid an unusually rigorous suppression. Ginsberg recalled the harsh treatment of Cleveland police who began to make a habit of raiding coffee houses to bust up poetry readings: "They even came into a coffee shop on Euclid Avenue while I was here and lined us all against the wall at gunpoint," Ginsberg recalled.

Today, the spirit of levy inhabits Mac's Backs bookstore. Above the basement stairs, his angular vestige stares down from a poster reading "Legalize Levy," a reference to the late 1960s campaign against efforts to suppress free speech from the highest levels of county government. The bookstore's owner, Suzanne DeGaetano, was introduced to levy by poet Daniel Thompson, another Cleveland legend who once resided in Coventry. Thompson began organizing poetry readings at Mac's, including readings of some of levy's work. Inspired by levy and motivated to celebrate his legacy on the 20th anniversary of his death, she organized a gathering in 1988 to celebrate his work. The event also captured the spirit of independent publishing that he pioneered through his "mimeograph revolution," a reference to the machines that opened up whole new worlds for underground publishing. A number of subsequent "levy fests" have continued the legacy of levy's poetic inspiration over the years.

A decade after levy's struggles with Cleveland law, a similar spirit for self-publishing motivated Harvey Pekar to cash in his record collecting habit to finance the publication of his first 16 years of *American Splendor.*

Coventry, especially in the early years, provided a consistent backdrop for Harvey's life and interactions with people on the streets. Like levy before him, Pekar became a literary pioneer, one of the first to define the autobiographical comic.

Levy and Pekar both produced unique archives of street-level observations of Cleveland, one transcendental and the other existential. It is worth noting the importance that walking played in both writers' lives, offering a pace for the slow observations and accidental encounters that make the life of good stories or poems. Too poor to afford a car, levy wrote "Cleveland Undercovers" as a succession of stops along a rapid line. He wrote at a time when freeways and urban renewal projects were carving up neighborhoods and obliterating much of the unique history of an immigrant city. The book *Mimeograph Revolution* recalls how levy "loved the life of the streets and may have wanted to stay close to it in cities," a sentiment similarly conveyed by Harvey Pekar, whose issues of *American Splendor* each begin with "From off the streets of Cleveland…"

As I walked home at night after a screening of the documentary *American Splendor*, perhaps one of the best archives of Cleveland history that I've seen, I paused at a sewer grating to listen to Dugway bubbling its quiet way below and a verse from levy's "Cleveland Uncovers" popped into my mind:

Sometimes city
When I walk at night
I slip into your past or future

References:
Interview with Joyce Brabner appearing on 90.3 *Sound of Applause* July 23, 2015.
d.a. levy and the Mimeograph Revolution, edited by Larry Smith and Ingrid Swanberg, Bottom Dog Press in Huron, Ohio. 2007.

THE RAPID

Shaker To Asiatown:

The Bikepath Review

AMY HANAUER

I live in Shaker Heights, on a tree-lined street between the high school and the library, and I work in Asiatown, between the Thai restaurants and the board-ups. Some mornings, when the weather allows, I don an ugly helmet and some fluorescent accessories, climb on my beat-up old bicycle, and careen down the traffic-clogged, pothole-filled roads from my home to my office.

The morning ride goes from idyllic to pure grit.

The first mile takes me past three elementary schools, kids of all ethnicities with half-zipped backpacks being escorted by attentive crossing guards. I see beautiful houses with golden retrievers posing in landscaped yards. I ride over the footbridge at Lower Shaker Lake, where the heron who lives about a mile south sometimes slums. In the fall, I sometimes catch an impossibly indigo glimpse of water through orange and red leaves. One week of cool clear mornings, I see what my daughter used to call a baby moon, a wisp of a white crescent in the pale blue sky.

As I turn downhill, the ride gets more intense. I used to take South Park where I rode on a seemingly protected sidewalk-level bike path, until one day a car screeched into a parking lot without checking the path. I still have a weird scar on my stomach from braking in panic, taking a handlebar to my belly before falling. Now I take North Park—less pleasant because I'm right in the mix with the cars. There's white paint slapped down to create a bike lane, which I love, but the lane is often filled with leaves and debris. And the path disappears abruptly, forcing a merger into traffic while on a fast downhill. But if there's a safe way to get from Shaker to University Circle, I haven't found it.

I claim a car lane because of the aforementioned disappearance of bike space. Vehicles hate this, but if you stay smushed against the curb, they crowd you with their two tons of lethal mobile steel. At the bottom of the hill, about seven lanes of angry drivers converge, all late to work, the road rage palpable in the air. There's a mud-clotted swamp on the (bike-intended) left sidewalk under the bridge, or there's the road. Every possible bike space here boasts a thick layer of skid-inducing gravel, mixed with glass shards, dead squirrels or blackened banana peels.

I pass Cleveland School of the Arts, which I've watched go in, brick by sturdy brick, window by gleaming window. Knowing the poverty statistics, my heart never fails to lighten at the reminder that Cleveland kids get to be in this exquisite, creative building, walking distance from the white marble art museum and orchestra hall, in the shadow of the near east side's lone wind turbine.

I survive the crazy crossing from the bottom of MLK to where I can make a left onto the blissfully bikeable Euclid (blissful, that is, except for the gravel and chunks of concrete). The eastern blocks of Euclid, 105th to 85th, are dominated by the bustle of the Cleveland Clinic. Doctors and other health care workers—black, white, Indian, Asian, Latino, and in-determinate—stride purposefully between the buildings while uniformed guards supervise the intersections. There's always a lustrous new building rising up. The shiny pool, with perfectly spaced rocks and slim saplings, looks like it was inadvertently plonked in grimy Cleveland instead of its intended office park in Singapore or Toronto.

Past the clinic, I frequently see other riders. Biking is often portrayed as a luxurious hobby of rich, white hipsters, bike infrastructure dismissed as more about luring wealthy trust-funders than supporting long-time city-dwellers. But if you actually ride around Cleveland, that notion is quickly put to rest. Sure, some fit, young, Lycra-clad men might breeze past me on slick Cannondales. But easily half the other bikers I see on or near Euclid are down-on-their-luck guys flashing a gap-toothed grin, people who seem like their dilapidated bike might be their only vehicle.

At one corner I see a gray-bearded man pushing a shopping cart piled high with cans and bottles he's collected, presumably to sell for recycling, and I cringe as the cart tips over—twice—while I wait for a break in traffic.

Aside from the scrum where MLK, Stokes, and Carnegie collide, my most dreaded part of the ride is the train bridge at Euclid and E. 55th. The thing about overhead train tracks is that there's almost always some-thing dripping from them. You try not to think about what. That traffic light is rarely in my favor, forcing me to wait under the overpass as filthy trucks and cars speed by, spewing exhaust and splashing toxic puddles in my direction.

When the light changes, though, I cruise the last few blocks past the Salvation Army where the clothes are arranged by color, purple turning to cobalt, turquoise, green. A telephone post advertises DNA testing, a warehouse advertises space available. Finally, I go right on 40th, through Chester, left on Perkins, and coast into the parking lot of my building, where the think tank I run, Policy Matters Ohio, is headquartered, alongside notable tenants like a parenting center for formerly incarcerated men, a homelessness coalition, the musician's union, an Asian social services center, a web design firm, a compost collection cooperative, and an artificial plant distribution operation. We share a love for the low rent, the enormous windows, and the friendly maintenance guys, Joe and Eric, who patiently field our news alerts about leaky roofs, malfunctioning heat, and mysterious carbon monoxide odors.

The ride home is the opposite, from urban to tranquil. Occasionally I come east on Hough, Central, or Quincy, which is fun because, especially at dusk, there are kids outside the housing projects, impressed with my multicolored wheel lights, shouting out their surprise that a white woman is biking by.

But usually I come back up Euclid with its reassuring bike lanes. I pass the Agora Theater, lines of pale concertgoers in black tees, heavy tattoos, and prominent piercings. I see Pierre's ice cream factory, a Domino's sugar plant, and Gallucci's.

I go by an abandoned board-up with a large plastic roaring lion and a sign reading "Coliseum Entertainment Center." Fence ignored, there is sometimes a trio of guys sitting on the shady front steps of the building at night, enjoying the scenery and calling out encouragement as I pedal by. Further up: two more board-ups that must have once been fast food restaurants. Some low-budget urban renewal inspired them to be painted over, boards and all—one a garish lavender with darker purple trim (now with a graffitied "Peace" in bubble letters), the other a brown, orange, and red combo, perhaps carefully chosen for how it clashes with lavender. One night recently, I was amused to see someone touching up the colors.

There are at least seven churches on my ride and two mosques. If there's a temple, I haven't noticed. One church sign reassures, "Do not let your hearts be troubled and do not be afraid."

The clinic is still a hive of activity in the evening. One night someone calls my name: a friend from Puerto Rico, smoking out front with her nephew, on break from visiting her husband being treated inside. Further up, a girl in Catholic school plaid with braids in every direction chatters away, hand-in-hand with her hospital scrubs-clad mother, who tiredly scans the horizon for a not-yet-visible bus.

Coming up the path between MLK and Stokes, I once, I'm convinced, saw a red fox; some urban naturalist can rate the plausibility of that claim. I still look for him every ride. That stretch feels like heaven: the hardest pedaling of the day, a steep uphill, with rolling green grass on either side. Then I turn left onto a busy street with a two-lane sidewalk-level path, happily separate from the cars. On the right is the stunning century-old Baldwin Water Treatment Plant, rows and rows of windows in a cream-brick building so narrow you can see through both sets of glass to the lowering sun behind. To the left are deep woods, descending toward the hill I just worked so hard to climb. It's a tough street to cross, but shockingly there's a tiny light for bicycles, where you push a button to force the light change. I climb that hill, passing one more treacherous intersection and, on Fairhill, some of the prettiest housing in Cleveland: slate roofs, stone walls, barn-shaped garage doors.

Finally the hill levels and I turn right onto 127th, a blessedly car-free block of duplexes with double-decker porches where residents appear integrated by race and sexual orientation but where a pit bull mix on a leash seems like a requirement. This lively stretch spits me out onto Larchmere near a new Brazilian restaurant with a patio. Not one, not two, but three times when making that complicated turn I've seen my friend Kamla out front, enjoying happy hour. Kamla was raised in Jamaica, not Brazil, but in Cleveland you sometimes take what you can get for restaurants reminiscent of home.

After that, the coasting is easy. I turn onto the mostly carless streets in the tiny area between Larchmere and Shaker Boulevard. After crossing the RTA tracks, I see two sisters in the evening light, the younger furiously pedaling her own training-wheeled bike, pink handlebar sashes blowing in the wind, the older on roller blades frantically issuing orders from behind.

I pedal by hands-free down side streets until I turn into my driveway, sweaty and happy regardless of the season.

I run a think tank, so a voice in my head constantly narrates how policy change could reduce poverty, crime, and pollution, or increase vibrancy, opportunity, and sustainability. Compared to other places I've lived, northeast Ohio makes it hard to bike, walk, or take transit, though recent improvements make biking easier than it was a few years ago.

There are 1,001 policy reasons to bike. But they aren't why I do it. Instead, it's because of that glimpse of the lake or the moon or the setting sun. It's the sweetness of that tired mom, that toothless guy, that bossy little roller-blader. It's the rush of completing a steep hill climb, or the joy of coasting on a downhill stretch.

It's the bliss of knowing that I was actually here, in my city, of my city, on my bike. ◀

CONTRIBUTORS

PHYLLIS BENJAMIN has served on both sides of the academic spectrum for over 55 years, having gained distinction as an administrator, consultant teacher and classroom teacher for school districts and universities in Greater Cleveland.

MIKE BROIDA spent his first eighteen years eating pierogis on a shady, quiet brick street in Slavic Village. He currently lives in Boston, where he writes about books, travel and bicycles.

LEE CHILCOTE is a freelance writer and editor who has written for *Vanity Fair*, *Next City*, *Belt* and other publications. His essays and poetry have been published in literary journals such as *PacificReview*, *Oyez Review* and *Blast Furnace*. He is cofounder of Literary Cleveland.

MARYANN DE JULIO has been visiting Little Italy in Cleveland for over thirty years. She is a professor in the Department of Modern and Classical Language Studies at Kent State University.

SALLY ERRICO has lived in New York for more than 10 years, but she still looks at Lakewood real estate online. Her writing and editing has appeared in *The New Yorker*, *The New York Times*, *The Independent*, the *Observer*, and *Northern Ohio Live*, where she was the associate editor from 2002-2005.

MANSFIELD FRAZIER manages The Vineyards and BioCellar of Chateau Hough across the street from his home at E. 66th and Hough Ave. When he's not tending vines he writes on social and criminal justice for CoolCleveland.com and spends his Sunday evenings broadcasting The Forum on WTAM.

SANDY GRIFFTITH spent several years living adjacent to the Flats in Tremont and occasionally misses the late night bike rides through the empty streets, having since abandoned Cleveland herself. She now resides in Brooklyn, NY where she spends time doing cool things with data and biking through busy streets.

VINCE GUERRIERI is a journalist and author in the Cleveland area. Every time he visits League Park, he feels like George C. Scott looking out over the Carthaginian battlefield in "Patton."

When Cleveland weather and her job/life schedule allow it, **AMY HANAEUR** rides her bike past the lakes and parks of Shaker Heights to the warehouses and grit of Asiatown. With her husband, Mark Cassell, she raises two teenagers, and with an awesome posse of staff she runs the think tank Policy Matters Ohio.

HARRIETT R. LOGAN is the owner of Loganberry Books on Larchmere Boulevard, where she is a tireless advocate for literature, Larchmere and local economics.

JANICE A. LOWE grew up mostly in Lee-Harvard and lives in New York City. A poet and composer, she is the author of *Leaving CLE poems of nomadic dispersal* and composed the musical *Sit-In at the Five & Dime*, (words by Marjorie Duffield).

GREGGOR MATTSON is Associate Professor of Sociology at Oberlin College and Chair of the Program in Gender, Sexuality and Feminist Studies. He is the author of *The Cultural Politics of European Prostitution Reform: Governing Loose Women*, and articles about gay bars, gentrification, and social inequality. A native of Washington State, he moved to Northeast Ohio in 2008.

BENNO MARTENS was born and raised in Cleveland and still calls it home. An independent writer and professional urban planner, he enjoys exploring the city's diverse neighborhoods, checking out the ever-growing craft beer scene, and cheering on The Ohio State University Buckeyes and all of Cleveland's professional sports teams.

SALLY MARTIN has resided in South Euclid with her family since 2001, serving as the city's housing manager since 2008. In 2015, she started a blog about the city's much maligned school district, selexperienceproject.com.

BRAD MASI likes to walk, bike or hike up and down the Portage Escarpment in Cleveland Heights, as it gives a momentary illusion that he's still in Colorado where he grew up. When not wandering around aimlessly, Brad makes films, writes, and consults on sustainable community development.

PEET MCCAIN is the founder of The Full Cleveland, an all day excursion exploring the city from one end to the other twice a year. He is also the proprietor of the Ithaca Court Occasional House, a B&B in the Eco-Village section of the Detroit Shoreway neighborhood in Cleveland.

SAM MCNULTY first visited Ohio City with his parents and six siblings as a child. Years later, during his Urban Planning studies at CSU, he interned with the local development corporation and saw massive potential for this neighborhood. For the last 12 years he has enjoyed living, working and playing on West 25th Street where with his business partners he has opened 5 restaurants and brewpubs.

DIANE MILLETT was drawn to her lake house in North Collinwood 11 years ago after living in Cleveland Heights for 25 years. Recently she exchanged writing legalese as an HR attorney for writing essays and poetry when she isn't gardening, cooking, entertaining, traveling or watching sunsets from her patio.

KATHRINE MORRIS has had her roots in Glenville her whole life. She is still a Glenville resident and is currently the Neighborhood Engagement Specialist at Famicos Foundation and works in the neighborhood that she loves in a meaningful way.

GEORGE MOUNT is a new resident of Parma, although his interest in the city started while attending Padua Franciscan High School. When not at work as a business analyst at MetroHealth, he plays violin in the Parma Symphony Orchestra and blogs at georgejmount.com.

TOM ORANGE was born and raised in Berea, left town at 18 and, several cities and university degrees later, boomeranged back home and has been living in Brooklyn Centre since 2010. He's Jazz Director at WCSB 89.3 FM, co-founder of the educational-promotional group New Ghosts, and an active performer in the local rock, jazz and experimental music scenes.

MEREDITH PANGRACE grew up in the western suburbs of Cleveland, but for the last 10 years has been an active resident of the North Collinwood community. She has been the Design Director of *Belt Magazine* since it's inception. Her design studio, Map Creative, is located in her family's former lithograph shop in the St. Clair Superior neighborhood.

DON PIZARRO grew up in Euclid, where he began 24 consecutive years of Catholic education. He turned out just fine and currently lives in upstate New York, where he's worked for years trying to get a second piece into McSweeney's Internet Tendency.

WILLIAM RICKMAN grew up in in the Albany, New York suburb of Latham, spent 12 years in New York City, and moved to Cleveland in 2008. His initial plan to stay in Cleveland for one year and then move on has clearly failed. His interests include rowing, bees, travel, biking, food, live music, birding, reading, botany, and sleep deprivation.

DOUG UTTER has lived in a big white house in East Cleveland for the last ten years, surrounded by fauna (white tail deer, his tabby cat Spanky, a couple of groundhogs, and yes, a coyote) and within sight of the long derelict Warner & Swasey Observatory. He sometimes makes paintings in his dining room and usually writes articles and poetry in the kitchen; he was awarded the Cleveland Arts Prize for Lifetime Achievement in 2013.

TARA VANTA is enamored of Tremont's history and hopes that the neighborhood evolves in a way that respects its heritage, especially the people. She makes maps for a living, but is still figuring out where she's heading.

DAVID WILSON is a freelance illustrator and designer living in Stow, Ohio. When he is not trekking around the Cleveland area looking for fish, frogs and other wildlife he is illustrating for clients such as *The Atlantic, The Boston Globe, WWE, Belt Magazine*, and many more.

ACKNOWLEDGMENTS

The essays were edited by Martha Bayne, William Rickman and Anne Trubek; Meredith Pangrace is responsible for the design, and the cover and interior illustrations are by David Wilson. Nicole Boose oversaw production. Thank you to Michael Gill, Claire McMillan, Matt Stansberry, and Annie Zaleski for their contributions, as well as Greg Donley, Josef Arvidsson, Scott Stettin, Meredith Pangrace, William Rickman, and Krissie Wells for help with the Editors' Picks. A huge round of applause and gratitude goes to our sponsors: Cuyahoga County Arts & Culture, Cosmic Bobbins, Mac's Backs, Loganberry Books, The Bop Stop, Global Cleveland, Cleveland History Center, Western Reserve Land Conservancy, The Happy Dog, fire food & drink, The Nash on East 80th Street, and Neighborhood Solutions. Finally: thank you to the essayists for their contributions, their enthusiasm and their words.

ABOUT BELT

Belt Magazine publishes independent journalism about the Rust Belt. Online only, it launched in September 2013, and focuses on longform journalism, op-eds and first person essays of interest to the Rust Belt and beyond. Belt Publishing, founded in 2012, publishes non-fiction with a focus on the Industrial Midwest. Both the digital and book publishing arms of Belt are committed to carefully edited, complex writing. We believe in quality over quantity, community over analytics, and the importance of the Rust Belt. We rely on individual members to sustain us.

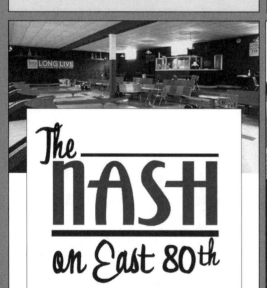

BELT
magazine

beltmag.com

Become a member